1 MONTH OF
FREE
READING

at

www.ForgottenBooks.com

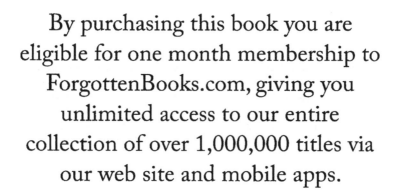

By purchasing this book you are eligible for one month membership to ForgottenBooks.com, giving you unlimited access to our entire collection of over 1,000,000 titles via our web site and mobile apps.

To claim your free month visit:

www.forgottenbooks.com/free908171

ISBN 978-0-265-90896-9
PIBN 10908171

ORNAMENTAL TREES, SHRUBS, AND WOODY CLIMBERS

During the past thirty-five years descriptive lists of best ornamental trees, shrubs, and woody climbers have been published from time to time in Experimental Farm reports, and the purpose of this bulletin is to bring these lists up to date, and together, under one cover, so that the person who desires to plant his grounds may have, in a convenient form, descriptive lists of the best species and varieties to use.

These lists are based on nearly forty years' experience with many kinds of plants at the Central Experimental Farm, Ottawa, Ont., and those recommended should succeed in most places in Eastern Canada where the climate is no more severe than at Ottawa.

How to Transplant a Tree or Shrub

When trees die after planting it is usually due to carelessness in transplanting. Some kinds of trees transplant much easier than others and some of those that are planted more commonly than others, such as the hard maple and American elm, are among the easiest to transplant, hence one is likely to become careless through success with these. Trees and shrubs should be dug as carefully as possible so as to retain a large proportion of the roots. The more roots there are the surer one is of getting the tree to live. The roots should not be allowed to become dry from the time of digging until the trees are in the ground again. They may be prevented from drying in transit by protecting them with wet moss or wet sacking. If the roots of evergreens, especially pines, become dry even for a short time the trees are almost sure to die. When planting, a hole should be dug large enough so that the roots may be spread out and not crowded or doubled up, and deep enough so that the tree or shrub will be from one to two inches deeper than it was in the woods or nursery. By planting a little deeper than it was before, provision will be made for a little heaving which often takes place the first winter, but planting too deep is almost as bad as planting too shallow. It is important to have the tree at least as deep as it was before digging and, as stated, best to have it a little deeper. The soil when thrown out of the hole should be put in two separate heaps, the surface or good soil in one and the sub-soil in another. If the soil is all poor, to get the best results some good soil should be brought to at least partially fill the hole. The tree is now placed in an upright position and the good soil is first thrown gently back about the roots of the tree. As it is important for the soil to come in close contact with the roots it should be trod firmly down with the foot, when thrown in. If there is not enough good soil available to fill the hole the poorer soil may be placed on top of the good. Manure should not be put in the hole with the soil as it may burn the roots and make the soil so loose that it will dry out easily. Better apply the manure to the surface of the ground in the autumn and dig in the shortest of it the following spring into the surface soil. After planting, the tree or shrub should be cut back well, the amount of heading in depending upon the amount of roots on the tree. If a large proportion of the roots are cut off a large proportion of the top should be removed, otherwise the large leaf surface will transpire so much moisture that the tree will dry up before the roots begin to take in more. This is why shade trees are cut back so severely when planted, but it is not necessary to reduce the trees to mere poles as is too frequently done, causing a bad crotch in the tree later on when the stub dies back and where rot is likely to get in. When large trees are transplanted it is desirable to steady them by tying to a stake or bracing them with guy ropes. Success is much surer when this is done.

44884—2

Evergreens are not headed back like deciduous trees as it would disfigure them too much and they have usually a fair supply of roots.

Before leaving the tree the surface soil should be loosened again so as to leave a thin mulch of loose soil on top which will prevent the moisture evaporating as rapidly as it would do if the ground were left hard. The surface soil should be kept loose throughout the summer and the best growth will be

Wier Maple *(Acer saccharinum wieri).*

obtained by keeping a circle of from two to three feet or more in diameter around the tree free of grass and weeds, where the soil will be kept loose and where the rain and air may find a ready entrance. If trees and shrubs are transplanted with care they should usually live. Early in the spring is the best time to transplant most kinds of trees and shrubs, evergreens included. Evergreens may be transplanted in summer but greater precautions must be taken to do it successfully and it is not recommended. Both evergreens and deciduous trees may also be planted in the autumn successfully, but on the whole they do not do so well as if planted in the spring.

Best Ornamental Deciduous Trees Hardy at Ottawa

In this chapter is given a list of best deciduous trees hardy at Ottawa, considered the most satisfactory of the large number of species and varieties tested since planting was begun on the Central Farm forty years ago. Many of those tested have not proved sufficiently hardy at Ottawa to be recommended, and others are not thought sufficiently attractive, but the following, unless otherwise stated, develop satisfactorily and are sufficiently ornamental for planting on private grounds or about public institutions.

Acer ginnala (Amur Maple).—Though usually resembling a shrub more than a tree, this small maple is one of the most useful ornamental small trees. No matter what the character of the season may be the leaves always turn red at Ottawa, and, while the season is rather short from the time the leaves turn until they fall, these trees are so effective at that time that they should be used more for colour effects. Moreover, this tree is quite attractive throughout the summer as the relatively small leaves give it a pleasing look. The seeds also have a rosy appearance while developing, which adds to the ornamental value of this little tree, which reaches only about 25 feet in height.

Acer negundo (Box Elder, Manitoba Maple).—The Box Elder may be considered a weed among ornamental trees, and often springs up where it is not needed nor wanted, growing very readily from seed. Because of its very rapid growth, this tree has been planted much more extensively than it should have been as it is very subject to insect pests, which render it unsightly by disfiguring the leaves and causing them to wither and fall prematurely. While the Box Elder may be planted in the colder parts of Canada because of the few kinds of trees which can be successfully grown, there is no need for it in most of Eastern Canada, where there are so many better trees available. Good specimens of this tree free from insects are, however, quite attractive in appearance, and the sight of such often tempts one to plant them, but, later on, experience proves that a mistake has been made.

Acer nigrum (Black Maple).—The Black Maple is closely related to the Sugar Maple, but is not as ornamental a tree as the latter. The leaves are downy, of a duller green, and do not colour as highly in the autumn as the Sugar Maple, but turn a pleasing shade of yellow.

Acer pennsylvanicum (Striped Maple).—The Striped Maple is a very interesting small tree because of the white stripes on the green bark of the trunk, which make it conspicuous. The large bright-green leaves also add to the attractiveness of this tree. It seems to succeed best in partial shade or associated with other trees rather than as an individual specimen in the open.

Acer platanoides (Norway Maple).—The Norway Maple has been much planted in Eastern Canada, and often it has been used when it would have been better to have planted the Sugar Maple, for it has no advantage over the Sugar Maple and is less useful in that it is not so hardy as the Sugar Maple and, unless very carefully pruned when young, the tree is liable to be low headed and to have bad crotches, and these, with winter injury, result in a breaking down of the trees when they are making fine large specimens. Furthermore, the leaves never turn red, always yellow, and, except for a contrast with the red leaves of the other Maples, this also makes them not so desirable. The Norway Maple grows rapidly, however, and makes an ornamental tree of considerable size. This tree thirty-five years planted is 44 feet high with a spread of 43 feet.

Acer platanoides schwedleri (Schwedler Maple).—There are many varieties of the Norway Maple, but the most useful and the most ornamental is the Schwedler Maple. This is very similar to the species in growth and habit of tree, but the leaves in the early part of the season are of an attractive shade of purple, making this variety very striking and ornamental. Later in the summer most of this purple disappears. This tree thirty-five years planted is now 44 feet high with a spread of 40 feet. In the variety *Reitenbachi*, the leaves, while duller in colour, remain purple all summer.

Acer rubrum (Red Maple).—Where one can grow the Sugar Maple successfully, one does not need the Red Maple, but, for low ground, where the Sugar Maple does not succeed well, it makes an excellent substitute. It usually colours more highly and earlier in the season than the Sugar Maple, and, where a colour effect with large trees is desired, this is a very useful tree. Its brilliant colour makes a fine contrast with evergreens in autumn. The Red Maple has a long range from north to south when growing wild and, if ordered from nursery firms for planting in the colder parts of Canada, one should be sure they have been grown from trees near the northern limit of their range, otherwise they are liable to winter injury.

Acer saccharinum (Silver Maple).—The Silver Maple is a very rapid-growing species and reaches a larger size than either the Sugar or the Red Maple. It is moisture-loving, and it is on bottom land or near the edges of streams where it usually reaches its greatest size. As it grows naturally in southern Manitoba, it is, next to the Box Elder, the hardiest of the Canadian tree Maples, but, if tried on the prairies, trees should be grown from Manitoba stock. It is the most graceful of all the Maples, the deeply cut leaves giving it a lighter look than the others. A pendulous form of this, the Wier Maple, *Acer saccharinum wieri*, is one of the most satisfactory large ornamental trees in Eastern Canada. It has been said that the branches of this tree break readily, and the trees become disfigured because of this, but this has not been the case at the Experimental Farm, Ottawa, where trees have been growing for thirty-seven years in an exposed position. This tree thirty-seven years planted is 66 feet high with a spread of 56 feet.

Acer saccharum (Sugar Maple).—The Sugar Maple is the best all round ornamental tree hardy at Ottawa. It is of attractive form, though there are trees more graceful in habit, but it gives the impression of strength and fitness both for planting in avenues as well as for single specimens or groups on the lawn. The foliage, as a rule, suffers little from diseases or insects, and, when the autumn tints are upon it, is very effective in the landscape and pleasing to the eye. When growing wild it is usually found in well-drained sandy loam soil, hence it is not desirable to plant it in low or poorly drained soil.

Acer tataricum (Tartarian Maple).—The Tartarian is not so graceful as the Amur Maple, and the leaves are not so deeply cut, but it is even hardier than the Amur Maple, though the latter is usually quite hardy except in the coldest parts of the Prairie Provinces, where it is sometimes considerably injured. On account of its greater hardiness, the Tartarian Maple is, therefore, more useful for the coldest places and, as the leaves colour highly, it is a very valuable small ornamental tree where the number of hardy species is limited. The variety *adjuense* has very highly coloured seeds.

Aesculus glabra (Ohio Buckeye).—This has made a fine attractive-looking tree at Ottawa, and has reached a height of about forty feet. While the flowers are not so ornamental as the Horse Chestnut, it is much hardier, the leaves are healthier, it fruits abundantly, and is altogether a desirable small ornamental tree.

Avenue of Cutleaf Weeping Birch, Central Experimental Farm, Ottawa, Ont.

Aesculus hippocastanum (Horse Chestnut).—The Horse Chestnut is not quite hardy enough to make a satisfactory tree at Ottawa, although some trees do very well when young, but seldom reach a great age. As it is a very handsome tree when in bloom, it is worth trying in protected situations on a large place, but is not recommended where one has space for but a few trees.

Amelanchier laevis (Allegheny Shadbush).—The Shadbush, of which this is considered the best species of those which take tree form, are useful for giving bloom early in the spring when few trees are in flower, they being literally covered with white flowers before the leaves open. The Downy Shadbush, *Amelanchier canadensis*, is also of tree form, and blooms freely, but is not as graceful a tree as the other. These trees are also known under the name of Shadblow, Juneberry, Serviceberry, and Saskatoon.

Betula alba laciniata (Cut-leaf Weeping Birch).—The Cut-leaf Weeping Birch is very effective as a specimen on the lawn, the deeply cut leaves and pendulous branches giving it a very light and graceful appearance. It is very hardy and succeeds in most places where tried in Canada. Unfortunately, there is an insect, the Bronze Birch Borer, which attacks the wood, causing the branches to die, and where this is troublesome it renders the trees unsightly. There is no practical remedy for this once the tree is badly infested, but, if the branches affected are removed and burned as soon as noticed, it may be checked. This tree thirty-eight years planted is 48 feet high with a spread of 38 feet.

Betula alba pendula youngi (Young's Weeping Birch).—This is a very attractive form of Weeping Birch and quite different in habit from the Cut-leaf Weeping Birch, being more spreading and lower growing.

Betula papyrifera (Canoe Birch).—This native Birch, associated with evergreens, is a familiar sight in a Canadian landscape, and the effect of the white and yellow paper-like bark of the trunks and branches against the green of the evergreens is very pleasing. As a single specimen on the lawn, however, it is not especially desirable as the frequent dropping of small dead twigs litters the lawn and makes their removal necessary, as is the case also with the Cut-leaf Weeping Birch. Because of its hardiness, however, it is particularly valuable in the colder parts of Canada.

Catalpa hybrida (Tea's Catalpa).—This is a hybrid between the Common and the Japanese Catalpas, and at Ottawa has proven as hardy as the Japanese and, as the flowers are more ornamental than the latter, may be grown in preference to it, and would seem more reliable for planting than *C. speciosa.*

Catalpa kaempferi (Japanese Catalpa).—While the Japanese Catalpa is not as ornamental a tree when in bloom as the Western Catalpa, the flowers being yellowish and relatively small, it has the large conspicuous leaves of the Catalpa, making it a striking specimen on the lawn. Moreover, it has proven hardier than the Western Catalpa at Ottawa.

Catalpa speciosa (Western Catalpa, Hardy Catalpa).—Some specimens of this Catalpa have proven quite hardy at Ottawa while others have been more or less injured by winter, much depending on the source of the stock. It is very desirable, therefore, when obtaining trees. to endeavour to get the hardiest stock. The Western Catalpa makes a very striking-looking tree of rapid growth, and the large, showy, white-and-purple flowers, which appear during the latter part of June, are a fine sight. The very large leaves also help to make this tree give a semi-tropical effect to the landscape.

Celtis occidentalis (Hackberry).—The Hackberry is a native tree, which is not very well known. It grows wild as far west as Manitoba. When given room it makes a spreading tree, of attractive form. The leaves are somewhat like those of the Elm, but are oblique at the base.

Cercidiphyllum japonicum (Katsura Tree).—This attractive-looking tree has proved quite hardy at Ottawa. It is closely related to the Magnolias, though has not conspicuous flowers. The leaves are heart-shaped, and, being rather small, give the tree a very light appearence, which not many large trees have. It is of broadly pyramidal habit and much branched. This tree thirty-five years planted is 44 feet high with a spread of 43 feet. The Katsura Tree is a very interesting tree and is the only species in the genus.

Katsura Tree *(Cercidiphyllum japonicum)*

Cladrastis lutea (Yellow Wood).—It is rather surprising that this small, graceful tree has been so little planted in Eastern Canada. It has proved perfectly hardy for many years at Ottawa. When it is in bloom during the latter part of June the long, loose, drooping panicles of white flowers are very effective.

The foliage, which is bright green, is attractive also. The tree is somewhat suggestive of a white-flowered Laburnum. It is one of the most desirable small trees. This tree thirty-five years planted is now 32 feet high with a spread of 23 feet.

Crataegus coccinea (Thicket Hawthorn).—There are many species of Hawthorns hardy at Ottawa, but those having attractive flowers, foliage, and fruit are among the most desirable. This is a native species which is quite useful for mixed plantations, and is singled out for mention here as it is so easily obtained.

Crataegus crusgalli (Cockspur Thorn).—The glossy leaves of this Thorn make it especially attractive and, while very thorny, this is expected in Hawthorns. The Cockspur Thorn makes a good hedge plant. This tree thirty-five years planted is 25 feet high with a spread of 23 feet.

Yellow Wood *(Cladrastis lutea).*

Crataegus oxyacantha (English Hawthorn).—The double pink-and-red flowered varieties of this Hawthorn are very attractive and, while they are not quite hardy at Ottawa, if planted in a protected place, some flowers may be obtained.

Elaeagnus angustifolia (Russian Olive).—Trees with greyish or silvery foliage are desirable for giving variety in ornamental planting, and this small tree is one of the best for this purpose. As its latin name indicates, it has narrow leaves. This tree thirty-five years planted is 30 feet high with a spread of 31 feet.

Euonymus atropurpureus (Wahoo).—It is difficult to decide whether certain plants should be classed as small trees or shrubs. The Wahoo, however, as grown at Ottawa, developed into tree form, and might be considered a small tree. It is a desirable tree to plant because of the ornamental fruit, which becomes crimson in autumn. The leaves, also, have attractive autumn tints. This has reached a height of about 18 feet at Ottawa.

Fagus americana (American Beech).—One seldom sees a native Beech tree on a lawn, but, given room to develop well, it makes a very fine specimen and, where one has spacious grounds and room for several large trees, at least one should be planted. The Purple Beech, which is a variety of the European Beech, kills back to the snow-line nearly every year at Ottawa, hence is not desirable.

Fraxinus americana (White Ash).—This is the most ornamental species of Ash. The tree is shapely, the foliage attractive in appearance throughout the growing season, and in the autumn has a purplish tint, which is very pleasing. It would make a good street tree but that the leaves are late in coming out and fall rather early in the autumn.

Fraxinus lanceolata (Green Ash).—The Green Ash is hardier than the White, though both succeed well at Ottawa. The glossy, bright-green foliage makes this a useful and attractive tree for a mixed plantation, but it is not quite good enough in form as an individual specimen.

Gymnocladus dioica (Kentucky Coffee Tree).—The Kentucky Coffee Tree is a very distinct species, and is useful where one has plenty of room and desires a great variety of tree forms. It is one of the more southern trees hardy at Ottawa. It makes few small branches, however, and when the foliage is off has a rather unattractive appearance. When in leaf, however, it is very striking. The long seed-pods, which are very conspicuous, add to the interest of this tree. The leaves come late and fall early, which are disadvantages. This tree planted thirty-five years is 37 feet high with a spread of 24 feet.

Halesia tetraptera (Silverbell).—This is a small tree or shrub, not quite hardy enough at Ottawa, though sometimes blooming well. The white, pendulous, bell-shaped flowers, which come in early spring, make it quite attractive at that time. The Mountain Silverbell, *H. monticola*, has not been thoroughly tested at Ottawa and may prove more hardy.

Hicoria ovata (Shagbark Hicory).—The Hicory is a rather slow-growing tree, but makes, eventually, a very handsome specimen, and seems to suggest the strength or toughness of wood, for which it is noted, in its general appearance. The glossy, deep-green foliage gives it a clean appearance also. A hicory tree will be much appreciated by the family for its nuts and at the same time will add to the appearance of the home grounds. This tree twenty-five years planted is 45 feet high with a spread of 32 feet.

Juglans cinerea (Butternut).—The Butternut is quite an attractive-looking tree when young, but later on is not quite leafy enough when grown as an individual specimen. On a large place, however, it may be planted, a Butternut tree being a great delight to the young people as the nuts can scarcely be surpassed in flavour. This tree planted about forty years is 43 feet high with a spread of 47 feet.

Juglans nigra (Black Walnut).—The Black Walnut, while not a species for small places, makes an attractive-looking tree, and succeeds very well in the warmer and well-drained soils at Ottawa.

Juglans sieboldiana (Japanese Walnut).—This is a very rapid-growing spreading tree, which makes a fine lawn specimen, but, like the Black Walnut and Butternut, the leaves come late and fall early. On large grounds, however, a tree of this species is desirable and is more attractive than either the Black

Walnut or Butternut because of its more abundant foliage. The nuts, however, are not as good as the Butternut. This tree planted thirty-five years is 37 feet high with a spread of 51 feet.

Liriodendron tulipifera (Tulip Tree).—Although this fine tree is a native of southwestern Ontario, it is not very satisfactory at Ottawa, killing back in severe winters, but the foliage is ornamental, and, where one has room, one might plant this tree in a fairly sheltered place, and thus add to the variety on the lawn.

Magnolia acuminata (Cucumber Tree).—The Cucumber Tree, if obtained from near its northern limit, proves hardy at Ottawa. While not particularly ornamental, it is interesting to have a specimen as it is the only Magnolia which has proved hardy. The flowers are not conspicuous, as are those of most of the Magnolias, being greenish tinged with yellow, and not noticeable at a distance. This tree planted thirty-five years is 30 feet high.

Bechtel Crab *(Malus ioensis plena)*

Malus baccata (Siberian Crab).—Its great hardiness and freedom of bloom make the Siberian Crab a valuable ornamental tree and, where it is desired to have a tree of one of the cultivated varieties of crab apples for culinary purposes, one might very well plant one of the best of these, such as Transcendent and Hyslop, and have something both useful and ornamental. They are highly ornamental both in flower and fruit. This tree thirty-five years planted is 28 feet in height and has a spread of 40 feet.

Malus ioensis plena (Bechtel Crab).—The Bechtel Crab is one of the most beautiful, hardy, small trees when in bloom. It flowers later than most crab apples or apples, usually being at its best during the last week of May to early

June at Ottawa. The flowers are large and double and of a delicate shade of pink and, with their exquisite perfume, are among the most charming flowers. The tree is not particularly ornamental after blooming, hence should be planted where it will not be very noticeable after flowering but where it will be most effective when in full bloom. It does not set any fruit.

Malus niedzwetskyana (Redvein Crab).—This remarkable apple or crab apple has proven hardy at Ottawa and is a desirable ornamental tree. The leaves are reddish purple, the flowers pinkish purple in colour, and the apples, though not useful for eating or culinary purposes, are very interesting in that the flesh is heavily stained with reddish purple. The habit of the tree is not very good, hence it should be planted where the foliage and flowers will be seen but where the tree itself will not be very conspicuous.

Phellodendron amurense (Amur Cork Tree).—This tree has proved hardy at Ottawa, and is interesting and fairly attractive in appearance, somewhat suggesting a Black Walnut in leaf.

Phellodendron sachalinense (Sakhalin Cork Tree).—A more attractive looking tree than the Amur Cork Tree at Ottawa, and quite desirable for planting when one is making a collection of hardy species.

Platanus occidentalis (American Plane Tree).—The European Plane Tree is much used for street planting in some of the large British and European cities and in some parts of the United States, but this species is not hardy at Ottawa. The American Plane Tree, however, though killing back somewhat at the tips is fairly hardy, and the Colorado form especially has developed into a striking looking tree of considerable size. The leaves are large and, though they are very late in appearing, this tree, being about the last to leaf out at Ottawa, arouses much interest, and the natural peeling of the bark adds to this. This tree planted thirty-five years is 48 feet high.

Populus angustifolia (Narrow-leaf Cottonwood).—This native Poplar makes quite an attractive lawn specimen. Unless familiar with it, one might not, at a distance, take it for a Poplar, the narrow leaves giving it a very unusual appearance for a Poplar.

Populus eugenei (Carolina Poplar).—The Carolina Poplar has had several scientific names, and the one used here is that adopted in "Standardized Plant Names." This handsome, strong-growing, leafy Poplar has been much used in Eastern America where a quick-growing tree is desired. It is supposed to be a hybrid. The Eastern Cottonwood, *Populus deltoides, var. monilifera,* is often called Carolina Poplar, but is not as ornamental a tree as *P. eugenei.*

Populus nigra italica (Lombardy Poplar).—The Lombardy Poplar is too well known to need much said about it. It is a most useful tree for accentuating certain effects in the landscape, its tall, upright form being very conspicuous wherever it is growing. As the centre of a group, as a single specimen behind or at the end of a building to give a tower-like effect, it helps to give character to the picture. It is very useful also in screening uninteresting walls and chimneys.

Populus petrowskyana (Russian Poplar).—The Russian Poplar under this name has proven to be the most satisfactory of the many Russian species and varieties tried. It is very hardy, a rapid grower, and makes an attractive, clean-looking tree.

Prunus maacki (Amur Cherry).—This is a very hardy cherry, the tree looking somewhat like a very large specimen of choke cherry and the flower clusters being also suggestive of the Choke Cherry. The tree is covered with these flowers in the spring, the tree at that time being very conspicuous. This is a useful tree on large grounds where striking effects with bloom are desired. This tree planted thirty-five years is 41 feet high.

Prunus padus albertsi (Albert Bird Cherry).—A very attractive, hardy form of the European Bird Cherry with large flower clusters grown in the greatest profusion. A good deal like the Choke Cherry, but a larger tree and with more abundant bloom.

Quercus imbricaria (Shingle Oak).—This Oak makes a small tree at Ottawa, and is usually quite hardy. The foliage is not dentated or cut as most

Effective group of Lombardy Poplar.

Oaks, but the leaves are entire, so that it is often not recognized as an Oak. The leaves are glossy and of an attractive shade of green. It makes an interesting lawn specimen, but should prove especially valuable where one wanted an effect in the shrubbery suggestive of Laurel as it resembles Laurel very much. It also makes a good hedge plant.

Quercus palustris (Pin Oak).—The Pin Oak has not done as well at Ottawa as the Red Oak, but there is at least one specimen which is all that could be desired. However, where its success is doubtful, it would be well to plant the Red Oak. The Pin Oak, because of its smaller and more cut foliage, is a more graceful tree than the Red, and the leaves colour very highly in autumn also. This tree planted thirty-five years is 41 feet high.

Quercus rubra (Red Oak).—The Red Oak is a very satisfactory tree. It is a relatively fast grower compared with some of the Oaks, being about as rapid a grower as the Sugar Maple. It makes a spreading tree of attractive form, the foliage is quite ornamental during the summer months, and in the autumn it turns to very effective shades of red. Moreover, the leaves remain on the trees a month or more after most other trees have lost theirs. Altogether it is one of

Red Oak *(Quercus rubra).*

the most desirable trees to plant where a large ornamental tree is desired, and is good as a street tree also, but must have abundance of space. This tree planted thirty-five years is 49 feet high with a spread of 53 feet.

Rhus typhina (Staghorn Sumac).—While becoming a small tree, the Staghorn Sumac is usually seen in shrub-like form as it suckers very freely and does not, as a rule, live long as a tree. It is a very useful tree for planting in dry or rough places for ground cover as it is attractive in summer and early in the autumn the leaves take on very brilliant hues, making a particularly effective feature in the landscape.

Robinia pseudoacacia (Common Locust).—The Common Locust is quite an attractive tree in form, foliage, and flower, and grows rapidly. It has, however, some defects and, as there are many good species to choose from, it is not one that is recommended for general planting. Its defects are that it is thorny, very subject to borers, and many seedlings are likely to grow, from seed scattered, over a wide area, making it become a nuisance. The suckers also are sometimes troublesome.

Salix alba x fragilis (Niobe Weeping Willow).—This seems identical with the Golden Weeping Willow as grown at Otttawa, and is one of the best weeping trees.

Salix blanda (Wisconsin Weeping Willow).—The Wisconsin Weeping Willow is satisfactory at Ottawa, but it is not as attractive in appearance as the Golden Weeping Willow or the Niobe Willow.

Shingle Oak *(Quercus imbricaria)*

Salix pentandra (S. laurifolia) (Laurel Willow).—The Laurel Willow is a rapid growing, ornamental tree, which is very useful on large grounds. It becomes a large tree. The leaves are deep green, glossy, and suggestive of Laurel. It is one of the most attractive looking Willows. Occasionally red spiders disfigure it at Ottawa. This tree planted thirty-five years is 52 feet high.

Salix vitellina pendula (Golden Weeping Willow).—This is the most satisfactory and attractive Weeping Willow at Ottawa. The graceful, weeping habit of this tree, combined with the yellow bark, make it very ornamental. It becomes a large tree.

Sorbus aucuparia (European Mountain Ash).—The European Mountain Ash, or Rowan Tree, as it is so often called, is one of the most ornamental small trees. It is hardy, a rapid grower, graceful in form, and, when in bloom and fruit, particularly attractive. The berries, unless eaten by birds, remain ornamental well up to winter. Where one has room for very few small trees this should be one of them. It is, however, sometimes affected by borers, by fire blight, and by sap suckers, but, even with these enemies, it is well worth planting. This tree thirty-five years planted is 38 feet high with a spread of 40 feet.

Sorbus decora (Showy Mountain Ash).—There are three native species of Mountain Ash, *S. americana, S. sambucifolia,* and *S. decora,* but the last is the most ornamental, and compares very favourably in that respect with the European Mountain Ash, and is hardier than the last, which, however, is not important except for the Prairie Provinces. The fruit, however, of this native species ripens before the European and the trees are soon denuded of it by birds in migration, hence where one wishes to have the fruit remain longer it is better to plant the European, which is a larger tree also than the native. This tree thirty-five years planted is 39 feet in height with a spread of 32 feet.

Niobe Weeping Willow

Sorbus pekinensis (Chinese Mountain Ash).—A closely related species to *S. americana* with pinkish fruit, which makes an interesting contrast with the scarlet-fruited species.

Syringa japonica (Japanese Tree Lilac).—This is a very satisfactory small tree or shrub as it blooms late, and is tall and effective on the lawn when it is in boom about the end of June, and is a mass of creamy-white flowers, which, however, have not the perfume of the common Lilac. Trees at the Experimental Farm, Ottawa, after being over thirty-five years planted are over 20 feet high. The Manchurian Lilac, *Syringa amurensis,* is very much like it. This tree thirty-five years planted is 21 feet high with a spread of 24 feet.

Tilia americana (American Linden).—The American Linden or Basswood is a large, spreading native tree, which is very effective on extensive grounds. Where one is limited for space, however, because of its spreading habit it is not so desirable. The foliage is often disfigured by insects, which is also somewhat against it where one is limited to a few trees. This tree planted thirty-five years is 40 feet high.

European Mountain Ash *(Sorbus aucuparia)*

Tilia cordata (Little Leaf European Linden).—Because of the small size of its leaves and its graceful form, this is, perhaps, the most attractive of the European Lindens. It has proven hardy at Ottawa so far.

Tilia platyphyllos (Big Leaf European Linden).—This European Species has grown well at Ottawa, but does not seem any more desirable than the native

American Basswood, and may not live as long. The variety *vitifolia* is a more attractive form than the species.

Tilia vulgaris (Common Linden).—The Common Linden is succeeding very well at Ottawa as a relatively young tree, but may not reach a great age. It is safer to depend on the American Linden.

Ulmus (European Elm).—The European Elms have, on the whole, not proved satisfactory at Ottawa. They continue growing too late in the season and are split by frosts or killed back. The Camperdown Weeping Elm, however, does fairly well.

Ulmus americana (American Elm).—This fine, graceful tree is too well known to need much commenting upon here. Large specimens of the American Elm are well known landmarks throughout Eastern Canada and the United

Siberian Crab *(Malus baccata)*

States. It makes a fine avenue tree, and for best effect should be at least 50 feet apart in the row. It grows rapidly and when planted much less than this the trees will meet in comparatively few years. At 40 feet apart, the trees in an avenue at the Experimental Farm, Ottawa, planted in 1888, have been interlacing for some years. It should not be planted on narrow streets or near houses as the roots extend for long distances and are liable to do damage to buildings. This tree planted thirty-eight years is 72 feet high with a spread of 70 feet.

Ulmus pumila (Dwarf Asiatic Elm).—This is a rapid-growing small tree with small leaves, and makes a rather graceful specimen, and, where there is room for small trees other than those with conspicuous flowers, this Elm might be planted with good effect.

44884—4

Ulmus racemosa (Rock Elm).—The Rock Elm is a fine, rugged-looking tree, and is well worthy of a place on large grounds. The rather short pendulous branches and cork-like bark are very characteristic of this tree. This tree planted thirty-five years is 45 feet high.

OTHER DECIDUOUS TREES WHICH ARE CONIFERS

There are two deciduous trees which are conifers which should be mentioned as they are both very desirable.

Ginkgo biloba (Maiden-hair Tree).—This is not an evergreen conifer, but it is such a striking and attractive tree that it should be much more generally planted than it is. (See page 22).

Larix europaea (European Larch).—This has proved a very satisfactory Larch at Ottawa. (See page 23).

TEN BEST SMALL TREES FOR ONTARIO

Acer ginnala—Amur Maple.
Amelanchier laevis—Allegheny Shadbush.
Catalpa hybrida—Teas' Catalpa.
Cladrastis lutea—Yellow Wood.
Crataegus coccinea—Thicket Hawthorn.
Malus baccata—Siberian Crab.
Malus ioensis plena—Bechtel Crab.
Aesculus glabra—Ohio Buckeye.
Sorbus aucuparia,—European Mountain Ash.
Syringa japonica—Japanese Tree Lilac.

TEN BEST LARGE TREES FOR ONTARIO

Acer platanoides schwedleri—Schwedler Maple.
Acer saccharinum wieri—Wier Maple.
Acer saccharum—Sugar Maple.
Betula alba laciniata—Cut-leaf Weeping Birch.
Cercidiphyllum japonicum—Katsura Tree.
Fagus americana—American Beech.
Populus eugenei—Carolina Poplar.
Quercus rubra—Red Oak.
Tilia americana—American Linden.
Ulmus americana—American Elm.

    To these might be added the deciduous conifers, Ginkgo biloba (Maiden-hair Tree), and Larix europaea (European Larch).

Best Conifers Hardy at Ottawa

There are, in Canada, many beautiful native species of conifers, and, as is well known, great areas of coniferous forests exist in the Dominion. Many attractive species from other countries have also been found to succeed well, and yet comparatively little planting of evergreens has been done for landscape effects. Perhaps it is because Canadians are so familiar with them in the wild that they do not show more interest in cultivating these beautiful trees.

Whether one sees the majestic yet graceful outlines of the White Pine, grown as a single specimen on the lawn and clothed with branches to the ground, or massed together in groups and showing their straight, tall trunks, one cannot but be impressed by its great beauty; and this is but one of many attractive-looking species which can be grown successfully and effectively at Ottawa, and where the climate is somewhat similar.

Evergreen conifers are very useful in taking away much of the bleakness in the Canadian winter landscape. The evergreens give a sense of cheer, which would otherwise be lacking; and, as there are good dwarf varieties, these can be planted quite close to the house. There are few of the broad-leafed evergreens, used to take the place of conifers for evergreen effects, on the West Coast of the Dominion, and in some other countries, that are hardy in Eastern Canada.

The importance of evergreen conifers for windbreaks cannot be too much emphasized. In the Prairie Provinces, where there are no natural windbreaks, their value for this purpose is, perhaps, most appreciated, but wherever the winds are high or the cold severe, they afford much appreciated shelter for both man and beast.

Some of the best hedges are made of evergreen conifers. These help to soften the hard lines about a residence which a Canadian winter does so much to emphasize where there are no evergreens.

Savin *(Juniperus sabina)*

Many species and varieties of conifers have been tested at the Central Experimental Farm, Ottawa, since the first planting was done some thirty-seven years ago. Of the number tested a large proportion have proved hardy. It is much to be regretted that the graceful Lawson's Cypress, of which there are many attractive varieties, is not hardy in Eastern Canada, nor the Cedar of Lebanon, Deodar Cedar, Redwood, Sequoia, and many fine Spruces and Firs which succeed so well in the coastal climate of British Columbia, but, in the following list of best conifers hardy at Ottawa, will be found many fine ornamental trees.

44884—4½

Abies balsamea (Balsam Fir).—The deep green, glossy foliage of the Balsam Fir makes this native tree quite attractive when young, but it should not be planted where it is desired to have an ornamental tree for many years as the experience at Ottawa has been that it is only while the tree is under twenty years of age that it is attractive. After that it becomes more ragged-looking, and eventually becomes so unsightly that it has to be removed. Used as a temporary tree among other trees, it has a useful place.

Abies concolor (White or Silver Fir).—The White Fir, though sometimes losing its terminal buds, has done well at Ottawa. It is often mistaken for the Colorado Spruce in the distance as the bluest forms are almost or quite as blue as that species. The tree is more pleasing in outline than the Colorado Spruce.

Abies lasiocarpa (Alpine Fir).—This tree is more compact than the Balsam Fir, and from experience at Ottawa would seem to remain attractive for a longer time. It is native of the Rocky mountains and varies considerably in hardiness. It is important to plant trees which have come from a source where climatic conditions are most like those in Eastern Canada.

Colorado Spruce, Austrian Pine and Pyramidal Arborvitae at the Central Experimental Farm, Ottawa.

Abies sibirica (Siberian Fir).—Like the Balsam Fir, this tree is more attractive when young than later on, but, as it is hardy and more distinct in appearance, it is well worth planting as a temporary tree where one has room for a collection of evergreens.

Ginkgo biloba (Maiden-hair tree).—This is not an evergreen conifer, but it is such a striking and attractive tree that it should be much more generally planted than it is. The leaves remind one of the Maiden Hair fern. While not particularly graceful, being of rather upright growth, it is very pleasing to the eye, owing to its remarkable fan-shaped foliage. While a rather slow grower, it is used as an avenue tree in some places in the United States with very good effect, and is quite hardy at Ottawa where trees are now about 35 feet in height.

Juniperus communis (Common Juniper).—There are many varieties of this Juniper, but the variety *depressa*, native of Eastern Canada, is the most satisfactory. This, like the Savin, is low-growing, and is useful for covering banks or for planting on rough, dry, stony ground, where an evergreen cover is desired. There is a golden-leaved variety, *aurea*, which makes a rather attractive contrast. If they were hardy at Ottawa, the upright forms of the common Juniper, namely, the Irish and Swedish, var *suecica* and var. *hibernica*, would be desirable as they are very attractive, but the tips of the previous year's growth winter-kill so often and disfigure the plants so much that they are not satisfactory. The Swedish Juniper has proved a little hardier than the Irish.

Juniperus rigida (Needle Juniper).—The Needle or Japanese Juniper is one of the most graceful species. Though of upright growth, the tips of the branches are pendulous. The foliage is yellowish green and the whole tree very distinct in appearance. Planted in 1896, it is now about twelve feet in height at the Central Experimental Farm.

Juniperus sabina (Savin).—This is a very useful native Juniper. It is a low-growing, trailing species, of which there are several varieties, and especially valuable for planting on banks or massing in other situations. The varieties *cupressifolia* and *tamariscifolia* are two of the best, and vary in height from a few inches to three or four feet.

Juniperus virginiana (Red Cedar).—This is a native tree, but the foliage of the type is dull in colour, hence is not very satisfactory for ornamental purposes. The variety *elegantissima*, however, has yellow tips to the foliage, which make it quite attractive. It is also of more graceful form than the type. Another good variety is *Schottii*, the leaves of which are brighter green than the species.

Larix dahurica (Dahurian Larch).—The Dahurian Larch is very distinct from the three other species noted here, being of a very spreading habit, a great contrast to the European, which is of pyramidal form. It is well worth planting where one has room for a good collection of conifers. It is a rather slow grower.

Larix europæa (European Larch).—This has proved a very satisfactory Larch at Ottawa, trees which have been planted thirty-six years being still in good condition. It is a very rapid grower of pyramidal and somewhat pendulous form.

Larix laricina (American Larch, Tamarack).—While not as ornamental as either the European or Japanese Larch, the American Larch is well worth planting in a mixed plantation, and because of its great hardiness is especially useful in the coldest districts.

Larix leptolepis (Japanese Larch).—The Japanese Larch has done well at Ottawa. It is of more spreading habit than the European and quite distinct.

Picea canadensis (White Spruce).—The White Spruce has a very wide adaptability in Canada, and is found wild from the Atlantic coast west to the Rocky mountains. It varies much in the colour of the foliage, some forms being very blue in colour, almost equalling the Colorado Spruce, and it is of more pleasing habit than that variety. It is particularly valuable in the Prairie Provinces where the number of species of hardy evergreens is limited. Unfortunately, it is very subject to attacks from the Spruce-gall louse and budworm, which make it very unsightly unless they are kept under control.

Picea excelsa (Norway Spruce).—The Norway Spruce has been, for many years, the most popular Spruce for planting in Ontario either for ornament or for windbreaks. It is a very rapid grower, and, with this characteristic and its graceful form, it soon makes a very attractive object on the lawn, and quickly gives protection when used as a windbreak. The variety *pyramidata* is of pyramidal form, which makes a very handsome tree more compact than the type, and is very desirable as an individual tree on the lawn. The pendulous varieties are attractive when young, but are likely to become ragged after a time. Some of the best of the dwarf or semi-dwarf varieties, of which there are quite a number, are *compacta, Remontii, Clanbrasiliana,* and *pygmœa.*

Group of Norway Spruce *(Picea excelsa)*

Picea engelmanni (Engelmann Spruce).—The Engelmann Spruce looks somewhat like both the Colorado Spruce and the White Spruce. It is of more pleasing form than the Colorado Spruce, being of distinctly pyramidal shape. Some of the bluer forms compare very favourably with the latter. While young, this tree, like the Colorado Spruce, is well clothed with branches to the ground, and continued so at Ottawa for about thirty years, after which the branches died from the ground up even though the trees were in full sunlight.

Picea omorika (Serbian Spruce).—This Spruce is not well known in Canada, but it is one of the most ornamental hardy species, and, where one is planting several kinds, it should not be omitted. It is rather a slow grower, but the contrast in colour between the different sides of the leaves makes it very attractive, one side of the leaf being dark green and glossy and the other side having lines of white.

Picea pungens (Colorado Spruce).—It is the blue forms of this Spruce which have made it so popular as it is not of very attractive form, being rather stiff, but the steely-blue leaves of the variety *glauca* and the form known as *Kosteriana* are very attractive to most people. At Ottawa this tree looks very well for twenty-five or thirty years after planting, when the foliage of most of the trees begins to die from the ground up, and after a few years they become too unsightly to leave. This should be taken into consideration when planting so that when removed a tree will not make too great a gap. This species does well in the Prairie Provinces. When buying this Spruce, one should ask for the blue form as among seedlings there is a large proportion of green ones. The cheapest way to get good blue specimens is to buy small, mixed seedlings and grow them a few years and plant the bluest ones. They grow slowly, however.

Mugho Pine *(Pinus montana mughus)*

Picea schrenkiana (Schrenk Spruce).—Although the foliage is rather dull in colour, this is an attractive, hardy species, which should be planted where one has a collection of evergreens as it is quite distinct.

Pinus cembra (Swiss Stone Pine).—Although a slow-growing species, this is a very attractive Pine. It has foliage much like the White Pine, but is an upright grower and very suitable for a situation where an evergreen is desired which will not take up much space. Twenty-five years after planting a specimen at Ottawa it is only 6 feet in width at the base and 19 feet high.

Pinus contorta latifolia (Lodge-pole Pine).—While there are several Pines hardy in Eastern Canada which are more ornamental than the Lodge-pole Pine, it has proven a satisfactory Pine for ornamental purposes in the Prairie Provinces, at least when young, being more attractive than the Jack Pine, *Pinus Banksiana*.

Pinus koraiensis (Korean Pine).—This Pine has done very well at Ottawa and has proven quite hardy. It is suggestive of the White Pine in foliage but darker, and is of more compact habit and a slower grower. A tree planted in 1896 is about twenty-one feet high. It is very attractive in appearance, and should be more extensively planted for ornament.

Douglas Fir *(Pseudotsuga douglasi)*

Pinus montana mughus (Mugho Pine).—The Mugho or Dwarf Mountain Pine is one of the most useful, hardy species. It is of bushy habit, and is excellent either as an individual specimen or in masses. Trees planted thirty or more years ago are 19 feet high and 28 feet across.

Pinus nigra var. austriaca (Austrian Pine).—Next to the White Pine, the Austrian Pine is, perhaps, the most ornamental, hardy Pine. It is not so graceful as the White Pine nor are the leaves of as attractive a colour, but it makes an excellent single specimen or group on the lawn. It is one of the easiest Pines to transplant and does well under very trying, dry conditions or poor soil.

Pinus ponderosa (Western Yellow Pine or Bull Pine).—This is even more attractive than the Austrian Pine, especially while it is young. It has glaucous green and somewhat twisted leaves, and are three in a cluster. It has a massive look both when young and later, and it is well worth planting where one has room for several Pine trees. It is a native of the dry districts of British Columbia.

Pinus resinosa (Red Pine).—The Red Pine is a native species, which somewhat resembles the Austrian Pine, but it has not proved as ornamental, after the first few years becoming too open in habit to be very attractive.

Pinus strobus (White Pine).—One or more Pines should be on every home grounds where the area is large enough to have a few trees, and this native species cannot be surpassed by any of the others which are hardy enough to grow in Eastern Canada. It is better known as a timber tree than as one for ornamental purposes, but when it has sufficient space for the side branches to develop well it becomes one of the most graceful evergreens. Its leaves, which are of a lively green, do no become as dull in winter as some others. This tree makes an excellent hedge also at Ottawa, where it has been kept trimmed for thirty-four years.

Pinus sylvestris (Scotch Pine).—The Scotch Pine is a hardy, rapid-growing species, but is not so attractive in form as either the White or Austrian Pines, but where there is room for many evergreens it should be planted as the colour of the foliage and habit of growth are distinct from other Pines.

Pseudotsuga douglasi (Douglas Fir).—The Douglas Fir, a native of Western Canada, has done well at Ottawa, and, after thirty-five years continues to be one of the most attractive evergreen trees. It makes a very stately tree, and is more graceful in its habit than most of the Spruces and other hardy Firs. It is desirable to get the trees from the colder and drier parts of its range. Individual trees vary much in the colour of their leaves, some having a much more bluish tint than others. The Douglas Fir has proved very satisfactory as a hedge.

Retinospora pisifera (Sawara Retinospora).—The Retinosporas really belong to the genus *Chamaecyparis* or Cypress, but they are so generally known under the above genus that it is used here. *Retinospora pisifera* is fairly satisfactory at Ottawa, but, from time to time, the tips are browned by winter sometimes to a considerable extent. The variety *plumosa* is very ornamental, but it also is injured more or less, and is often rendered unsightly, and *plumosa aurea*, a very attractive variety where hardy, is also injured at Ottawa. The variety *squarrosa*, which is a fine sort when it is not browned by winter, suffers even more so. None of the above are really satisfactory. The variety *filifera* is, however, entirely satisfactory. It has not been injured at Ottawa in any way and has made a very graceful and beautiful lawn specimen. It has drooping branches and slender threadlike pendulous branchlets. Specimens thirty years or more planted are now about 18 feet in height. This is one of the best hardy evergreeens.

Taxus canadensis (Canada Yew).—The Canada Yew is a low-growing hardy species, which may be used with good effect for covering banks in shady places or as an undercover among tall trees.

Taxus cuspidata (Japanese Yew).—The English Yew, which is so common in Great Britain, is not hardy in Eastern Canada, but in the Japanese Yew there is a splendid substitute, which is perfectly hardy at Ottawa. A specimen planted in 1896 is now 10 feet high and 15 feet broad. It may be used with good effect for massing, or as single specimens; and for hedge purposes the foliage is attractive.

Thuja occidentalis (American Arborvitae).—The American Arborvitae is valuable both as an ornamental tree and for hedge purposes. It makes the best evergreen hedge at Ottawa. As it is a very common native tree in Eastern Canada, it is very easy to procure it at little or no cost. While the ordinary form is attractive, some of the cultivated or horticultural varieties are, at least, of more striking habit and give greater variety in the landscape. A large number of these have been tested at Ottawa during the past thirty-seven years,

Austrian Pine, Siberian Arborvitae, and White Pine.

but many have, in some winters, been injured. Some of those which withstand the climatic conditions at Ottawa best are var. *robusta* or *Wareana*, the Siberian Arborvitae, which seems to be hardier under cultivation than the typical form, and does better on the prairies than others. It is of compacter habit and has brighter green foliage than the species. The variety *globosa* is also very hardy, and makes an interesting shrub of globose form. This is a rather dwarf form, a specimen being only six feet in height after thirty-five years since planted. The variety *Ellwangeriana* is one of the most distinct hardy forms. It has small foliage, which gives it a soft appearance, and is of semi-dwarf habit, being only about fifteen feet high after over thirty years. The variety *Douglasi pyramidalis* is hardier than the better known pyramidal variety *fastigiata*, though it is not so columnar in form, but has distinct foliage. The pyramidal arborvitae, var. *fastigiata* or *pyramidalis*, makes a very striking object on the lawn or wherever placed. At Ottawa, specimens over 30 feet in height are only 6 feet across near the ground. A large proportion of the specimens planted thirty-five years ago have, however, been so disfigured by injury in some winters that they have had to be removed. However, others are still in good condition, and it is, on the whole, very satisfactory. Another variety which has remained in good condition in *Vervaeneana*. This has yellowish foliage but not a distinct enough yellow, but it is more graceful than the species. There are many other attractive forms, which, no doubt, would succeed better in milder parts of Ontario than at Ottawa.

Thuja plicata (Giant Arborvitae).—The Giant Arborvitae, which is native west of the Prairies, has been little planted in Eastern Canada. It is a beautiful species, the tree being of more graceful habit than the American Arborvitae and the foliage of a brighter green. Success in growing this tree will depend on the source of the stock as, if obtained from the milder parts of Canada or the United States, it is almost sure to winter-kill, or be badly injured, but if the stock comes from Montana or from a somewhat similar climate in Canada, where it is cold and relatively dry, it should do well and make a very attractive lawn specimen, as it has done at Ottawa.

Tsuga canadensis (Canada Hemlock).—This Hemlock, native of Eastern Canada, is one of the finest evergreen trees. It is very graceful in habit, and the small foliage is of a pleasing shade of green. Although it eventually makes a large tree, it grows slowly and it is a rather long time before it becomes very conspicuous on a lawn. When grown in the open also it is liable to be injured by winter. It does best when growing in the partial shade of other trees or on banks with a northern or eastern exposure. The variety *gracilis* is a charming tree with smaller foliage and of slower growth than the species. The Canada hemlock makes a very attractive hedge, and may be kept quite small because of its slow growth.

Best Ornamental Shrubs Hardy at Ottawa

Many species and varieties of ornamental shrubs have been tested at the Central Experimental Farm, Ottawa, and at the Branch Farms and Stations during the past forty years, and notes have been made on their hardiness and attractiveness of foliage, flowers, form, and fruit. The height to which they grow has also been recorded. There has been a great increase in interest in the beautifying of home grounds in recent years, and it is hoped that the following descriptive list of species and varieties found to be the best at Ottawa will prove of value to those who contemplate improving the appearance of their places. This list is mainly of species and varieties with ornamental flowers.

Amelanchier laevis (Allegheny Shadbush).—Eastern Canada and Eastern United States.—There are several native species of *Amelanchier* which bloom early in the spring and are very ornamental at a time when there are few kinds of shrubs in bloom. Some, such as *A. alnifolia var. pumila*, are quite dwarf, while others become small trees. Perhaps the most ornamental is *Amelanchier laevis*, also called *A. canadensis*, which, early in May, is covered with loose, drooping racemes of white flowers. The first leaves, which are developing at this time are purplish and make a pleasing contrast to the flowers. It reaches a height of from thirty to forty feet. Some of the June Berries have large fruit, which is of good quality. It is known in the Prairie Provinces as Saskatoon. Another common name is Service Berry.

Amorpha canescens (Lead Plant)—Southern United States.—An attractive summer-blooming shrub with divided leaves and small, bluish flowers on long, close spikes. It grows about 3 feet in height, and looks well on a bank or in any stony or rocky place. It blooms during June and July.

Atraphaxis frutescens (A. lanceolata)—Caucasus, Turkestan, Siberia.—
This is an attractive, low-growing, hardy shrub, flowering in summer the blooms
remaining attractive until autumn because of the calyx being persistent. It
belongs to the buckwheat family, the flowers are suggestive of those of buckwheat and are pinkish in colour.

Berberis thunbergi (Japanese Barberry)—Japan.—Height 2 to 4 feet.
The best barberry for ornamental purposes. It is a dwarf, compact shrub,
with bright green leaves in summer, changing in autumn to deep red. The
flowers, while not very striking, are attractive. The scarlet fruit is borne very
profusely and makes this barberry quite ornamental throughout the winter.
The purple or red-leafed variety is desirable.

Snowball Hydrangea. *(Hydrangea arborescens grandiflora)*

Caragana arborescens (Siberian Pea Tree)—Siberia, Manchuria.—The
Siberian Pea Tree is one of the most useful hardy ornamental shrubs for it is
really a shrub, though reaching a height of fifteen to eighteen feet or more. The
foliage is attractive, and the yellow, pea-shaped flowers, which appear while
the leaves are still young in May, make it a striking object during the spring.
Because of its great hardiness and its ability to withstand drought, it is particularly useful on the prairies as a windbreak and for hedge purposes. It makes
a very good hedge in Eastern Canada also.

Caragana frutex var. grandiflora (Large-Flowered Caragana)—Caucasus.—Height 4 to 6 feet. In bloom third week of May. Flowers large, bright
yellow, pea-shaped. Very pretty when in full bloom. This variety resembles
C. frutex, or *C. frutescens* as it is sometimes called, but has larger flowers than
this species. The bush is somewhat pendulous, which makes it rather graceful.

Caragana pygmaea (Dwarf Caragana)—Caucasus to Siberia and Thibet.
—This species of Caragana differs very much from the others, but has an
attractiveness all its own. It is a comparatively low-growing shrub of spreading
habit, reaching a height of about 4 feet. The leaves are of duller green and

narrower than either *C. arborescens* or *C. frutex,* and the flowers, which are in bloom in May, instead of being altogether yellow, are orange and yellow. This makes a neat, low-growing hedge plant, though the leaves are rather too dull in colour for best effect.

C. tragacanthoides resembles *C. pygmaea* very much, but is of looser-growing habit.

Chionanthus virginica (Fringe Tree)—Eastern and Central United States. —The Fringe Tree is usually really a shrub and one of the most interesting hardy species. It blooms in June after the flowers of most hardy shrubs are gone. The flowers are white and borne in long, loose panicles, and this, combined with their narrow petals, gives them the fringe-like look which suggests the name. Some shrubs bear only staminate flowers, and these are more ornamental than the others, as the panicles are larger. Specimens of this shrub are now about 9 feet in height at Ottawa, but where native it will grow from 25 to 30 feet high.

Smoketree *(Rhus cotinus).*

Clethra alnifolia (Sweet Pepperbush).—Eastern United States.—One of the latest-blooming shrubs, being in flower from July to September. It grows from 4 to 8 feet in height, and has small, sweet-scented, white flowers which bloom in compact racemes. This shrub succeeds best in rather moist soil. Another species, *Clethra acuminata,* is a taller grower, and is quite hardy at Ottawa.

Cornus alba sibirica (Siberian Dogwood)—Siberia, North China.—The Siberian Dogwood is attractive when it is in flower in late May or early June, but it is especially so in winter, when the bright-red bark is very striking. There is a yellow-barked dogwood called *Flaviramea* which looks well in winter in contrast with the red bark of the others.

Cytisus (Broom).—None of these is a very important flowering shrub in Eastern Canada, though a few of the lower-growing species are fairly hardy and quite ornamental. The hardiest is, perhaps, *Cytisus elongatus*, with bright but rather pale yellow flowers. *C. ratisbonensis* is very like it. These bloom in the latter part of May and are quite showy at that time. The bushes reach a height of about 3 feet.

Cytisus nigricans, which blooms in June and July, later than *C. elongatus*, is more ornamental than the latter, as the flowers are of a richer yellow and are in long, slender racemes, but it is not perfectly hardy at Ottawa and gradually kills out.

Another *Cytisus*, which blooms well every year, though the tips of the branches are usually killed back, is *Cytisus purpureus* and its varieties. This pretty shrub is low-growing, being 2 feet and under in height. The flowers vary in colour from light pink to purple. It is in bloom in May. A cross between this and *C. hirsutus*, namely *C. versicolor*, with pale-purple and light-yellow flowers, is trailing in habit.

Another low-growing species about 1 foot in height and very ornamental is *Cytisus purgans*. This usually blooms well and is practically covered with flowers of the rich yellow colour of the well-known Broom.

Daphne mezereum—Europe to Altai and Caucasus.—The very sweet-scented flowers of this shrub appear in the latter part of April, and are among the first spring flowers. The flowers are pink, but there is a white-flowered variety also. This shrub will eventually reach a height of about 4 feet.

A low-growing, almost creeping species, *Daphne oneorum*, is very hardy also, and is one of the most sweet-scented of flowering shrubs. The flowers are pink also.

Deutzia gracilis—Japan.—This is a charming little shrub, reaching a height of about 3 feet, blooms during the early part of June, and is a mass of white flowers. It is not so hardy as *Deutzia lemoinei*, which is quite hardy at Ottawa, though not so attractive as *D. gracilis*.

Diervilla hybrida.—One of the hardiest and most attractive of these at Ottawa is Eva Rathke. It begins blooming in June and continues throughout the summer. The flowers are very attractive and dark-red in colour. It grows from 3 to 5 feet in height. Most of the Weigelias are too tender at Ottawa. Some specimens of *D. rosea* are fairly hardy.

Forsythia suspensa (Golden Bell).—China.—The Golden Bell blooms before the leaves are out in the spring, and if the flower buds are not killed in winter the branches will be covered with yellow flowers. It is a graceful shrub of pendulous habit, reaching a height of 6 to 8 feet. Owing to the danger of the flower buds being killed in winter, it would be desirable to plant these shrubs where they will be out of the sweep of the wind. The hybrid variety, *F. intermedia*, though little, if any, hardier, is a very free bloomer, and its variety, *spectabilis*, has deeper-coloured flowers.

Genista tinctoria (Dyer's Greenweed)—Europe, West Asia.—Nearly all the *Genistas* winter-kill at Ottawa, but this species, which has deep-yellow flowers, though killing back a little, is fairly satisfactory, and individual bushes live for many years, reaching a height of about 3 feet. The variety, *elatior*, is somewhat stronger growing than the species. There is a double-flowered, almost creeping form, *G. tinctoria plena*, which is very attractive, especially for rockeries.

Halesia carolina (H. tetraptera) (Silver Bell)—Southeastern to Central United States.—The Silver Bell, or Snow Drop Tree, as it is sometimes called, does not make anything more than a shrub at Ottawa. In some years it is considerably injured by winter, while in others one is rewarded for growing this beautiful plant by having it bear, during the month of May, an abundance of drooping white, bell-shaped flowers, which are very conspicuous, as they open before the bush is fully clothed in leaves.

Halimodendron halodendron (H. argenteum) (Salt Tree)—Central Asia from Transcaucasia to the Altai.—The Salt Tree, which is really a shrub, grows from 5 to 6 feet high, and is especially valuable because it flowers late in June, after so many other shrubs are out of bloom. The flowers are lilac or pale pinkish-purple in colour and the leaves bluish-green. It is a very hardy shrub, and is succeeding well on the prairies.

Hydrangea arborescens grandiflora—United States.—Height 4 to 6 feet. A very free-blooming variety with large panicles of white flowers which come in succession from July to September. The bush kills back each year, but it is sufficiently hardy to ensure abundant bloom.

Hydrangea paniculata grandiflora (Large-flowered Hydrangea)—Japan. —Height 6 to 10 feet. Blooms remain attractive from August until October. Flowers white, gradually becoming pink, and borne in very large panicles. This is one of the finest hardy shrubs. To get best results the bushes should be pruned back severely every spring and given an abundant supply of water during the growing season.

Lespedeza sieboldi (Desmodium penduliflorum) (Bush Clover)—Japan. —This graceful plant is really not shrubby at Ottawa, as the branches kill to the ground every year, but strong stalks are thrown up from the ground each spring, and the shrub has usually a profusion of rosy-purple flowers in late September and early October. It is very graceful and attracts much attention when in bloom.

Lonicera tatarica (Tartarian Honeysuckle, Bush Honeysuckle)—Siberia, Tartary.—Height 5 to 10 feet. In bloom third week in May. Flowers bright pink. This is an old favourite and one of the hardiest shrubs grown. There are many varieties of this fine shrub and a large number of hybrids. These vary in colour of flower from white to rose. Some of them have yellow-coloured fruit. Among the best are: *L. tatarica pulcherrima*, with rosy petals, having pink margins; *L. tatarica gracilis*, flowers rosy in bud, pink and rose when open; *L. tatarica speciosa*, flowers large, pink and rose; *L. tatarica splendens*, flowers pink in bud, pink and white when open; *L. tatarica grandiflora rubra*, flowers rosy in bud, rosy with pink margin when open; *L. tatarica elegans*, flowers pure white; *L. tatarica alba grandiflora*, flowers white; *Lonicera morrowi*, with white flowers, is of more spreading habit, and is very ornamental also.

Mahonia Aquifolium (Oregon Grape or Holly-Leaved Barberry)— Canada and the United States.—Height 2 to 3 feet. A very attractive low-growing shrub. The leaves are very glossy above, and sometimes have a pleasing bronzy tint. The edges are toothed, and the leaf, on the whole, is quite suggestive of that of English holly. During the latter part of May this shrub blooms freely, there being numerous clusters of small, bright-yellow flowers. While this is an evergreen, the old foliage is usually browned and disfigured by winter unless protected with a little straw, but the new growth soon appears in any case and the old foliage is not noticed. It increases rapidly by suckers, and is excellent for underplanting in partially shaded places.

Philadelphus coronarius (Mock Orange or Syringa)—South Europe.—
Height 5 to 10 feet. In bloom second week of June. Flowers white with a
strong, sweet odour; a well-known popular shrub. In addition to this species,
there is *Philadelphus grandiflorus*, a taller and later blooming species, *P. grandiflorus speciosissimus*, several other species and many fine hybrid varieties, among
the best of which are: Virginal Bouquet Blanc, Nuée Blanche, Voie Lactée,
Atlas, Albâtre, Pyramidal. The golden-leaved variety of *Philadelphus coronarius* is one of the best hardy golden-leaved shrubs.

Physocarpus opulifolius (Ninebark)—Canada, United States.—This is a
rather large shrub, which is satisfactory in rather shady places or along streams.
It reaches a height of 8 to 10 feet or more and bears many white flowers in
clusters in June. It is often known as *Spiraea opulifolia*. There is a golden-
leaved variety of this, which makes a nice variety in the landscape if golden-
leaved shrubs are desired.

Japanese Tree Lilac *(Syringa japonica)*.

Potentilla fruticosa (Shrubby Cinquefoil)—Canada, United States,
Europe, N. Asia.—This is a native plant which succeeds well under cultivation,
and blooms continuously from June until autumn. The flowers are an attractive
shade of yellow. It grows from 2 to 4 feet high.

Prunus nana (Russian Almond)—Russia and West Asia.—The Russian
Almond is grown under the name of *Prunus japonica* and *Prunus nana*. It
blooms early in May; the flowers are pink in colour, and, though rather small,
are conspicuous, as the bush is not yet in full foliage when it is in bloom. There
are double-flowered forms, both pink and white, most of which may be referred
to *Prunus japonica*. The height of these shrubs varies from 3 to 5 feet.

Prunus tomentosa (Down-Leaved Cherry)—Japan, North China, Manchuria.—It is desirable to have as many points of merit as possible in flowering
shrubs, and this one is ornamental in flower and bears a useful fruit as well. It
blooms early in May. The buds are pink, though the petals are white when
they expand, and the calyx is red. It is a very hardy bush cherry. The fruit

is small compared with the cultivated sour cherries, but is excellent when canned. This shrub is very hardy, and has reached a height of about 10 feet at Ottawa.

Prunus triloba plena (Flowering Almond)—North China.—This double-flowered ornamental almond is one of the most attractive shrubs in spring, those on their own roots being the most satisfactory. When top-grafted on other stock, they frequently winter-kill, and at Ottawa are not at all satisfactory, whereas when grown in bush form they bloom abundantly year after year, and the double pink flowers, which are in bloom before the leaves are fully out, are very attractive and make this a striking looking shrub. Specimens at Ottawa have reached a height of about 10 feet.

Pyrus japonica (Japanese Quince)—China and Japan.—This shrub blooms very early, and has bright red flowers. It is somewhat tender, and should not be planted in a very exposed place. A hardier form of this is *Pyrus Maulei*. The former grows from 3 to 6 feet high, and the latter only reaches about 3 feet in height.

Rhododendron viscosum (Clammy Azalea or White Swamp Honeysuckle)—Canada and United States.—The hybrid rhododendrons are not satisfactory at Ottawa, and few of the species either, though, with special protection in winter, fine blooms have been produced on some of the good hybrids. There is one native species, however, formerly known as *Azalea viscosa*, which does well under ordinary conditions. The sweet-scented flowers are white, sometimes tinged with rose, and this is well worth growing where one desires an assortment of flowering shrubs. It blooms during June to July. Varieties of *Rhododendron japonicum* can also be grown successfully with a little protection.

Ribes aureum (Missouri Currant)—Canada, United States.—Height 6 to 8 feet. In bloom fourth week of May. Flowers yellow and very sweet-scented. This currant is quite ornamental, especially when in bloom; and again in summer, the fruit, which is quite palatable, makes it attractive.

Robina hispida (Rose Acacia)—Southeastern United States.—The rose acacia is one of the most attractive hardy shrubs. It blooms from June more or less throughout the summer, and the rosy-pink flowers are very conspicuous and ornamental. The foliage is attractive also. If not propagated on a non-suckering stock, it is liable to sucker considerably, but usually not sufficiently to be troublesome.

Rosa (Roses).—It is almost needless to write that the roses are among the most attractive shrubs. A separate paragraph has been given to two of the hardy species, but, in addition to these, there are such hardy shrubs as the Persian and Harison Yellow Roses, Austrian Briars, the Provence or Cabbage Roses, the Moss Roses, the Damask Roses, the Scotch Rose, and others. In Bulletin No. 17, New Series, on "Hardy Roses, Their Culture in Canada" will be found fuller particulars in regard to the many beautiful varieties that are now available.

Rosa rubrifolia (Red-Leaved Rose).—This is such a distinct shrub that it should be treated separately. The leaves are purplish red, making it a striking object during the growing season even when out of bloom. The flowers are rather small and deep pink in colour, and the fruit is bright red and shows up well after the leaves have fallen. It is very hardy, succeeding well on the prairies, and reaches a height of from 6 to 8 feet.

Rosa rugosa (Japanese Rose)—Japan.—Height 4 to 5 feet. In bloom second week of June. Flowers very large and deep pink. This is a beautiful rose with fine flowers and very ornamental leaves, which are large, thick, and shiny. There is a white-flowered variety which is also good, also a number of hybrids between *rugosa* and varieties of hybrid perpetual and tea roses, most of which are quite hardy.

Sambucus (Elder).—There are several species of Elder which make very satisfactory shrubs for growing near streams or rather moist places. One species, *Sambucus racemosa*, and its variety, *pubens*, blooms in May and has red berries and another one, *Sambucus canadensis*, blooms in June and July and has purple-black fruit. A variety of this, called *maxima*, has enormous panicles of flowers and is very showy. *Sambucus nigra*, an European species, corresponds somewhat to *canadensis*, but blooms earlier. The golden-leaved variety of Elder is very attractive to many.

Sorbaria sorbifolia (Spiraea sorbifolia)—North Asia from Ural to Japan. —A well-known shrub, growing from 4 to 5 feet in height. It is one of the most useful on account of its flowering in summer when most other shrubs and trees are out of bloom. The leaves, which resemble those of the mountain ash, very much, from which it gets its name of *sorbifolia*, are quite attractive at all times, but in spring are particularly so. This shrub blooms from late June until autumn, and its large panicles of white flowers make it a conspicuous object. Its fault is that it suckers badly and, on this account, should not be planted near anything which it is likely to crowd out. There is a taller-growing species, not quite hardy enough at Ottawa, which blooms later, namely, *S. aitchesoni*, the long branches of which should be bent down so that the snow will cover them in winter. If this is done, one is likely to have very fine panicles of bloom during late summer and autumn. This grows from 8 to 10 feet in height and is very ornamental.

Spiraea alba (Meadow Sweet)—Eastern to Central United States.—The Meadow Sweet is a native shrub which is very useful for ornamental planting, especially in damp situations. It grows from 4 to 5 feet high and flowers in summer when there are few shrubs in bloom. The flowers are small and white but borne in good-sized panicles. There are two other species very much like the last, namely, *Spiraea latifolia*, with larger panicles, and *S. salicifolia*, both with white flowers though sometimes pinkish in colour. A hybrid species, known as *Spiraea billardi*, is very similar to the above in habit, but has rosy-pink flowers.

Spiraea arguta—Europe.—Height 3 to 4 feet. In bloom third week of May. Flowers pure white, produced very profusely in compact clusters. This is the earliest flowering spiraea grown here, and is one of the best hardy shrubs of rather recent introduction. It is a graceful little spiraea with pendulous branches, but its chief beauty lies in the abundance of its pure white flowers.

Spiraea media—South East Europe to Japan.—One of the earliest-blooming hardy spiraeas flowering at the same time as *S. arguta*, but being much hardier. The bush is not as graceful as either the latter or *S. van houttei*, but, when in full bloom and well covered with the compact clusters of white flowers, it is very ornamental, and, being very hardy, is especially desirable for the prairies. This is sometimes found under the name of *S. oblongifolia*, which is a synonym of *S. media subintegerrima*, and little different from the type.

Spiraea van houttei (Van Houtte's Spiraea)—Europe.—Height 3 to 5 feet. In bloom first week of June. Flowers pure white, borne very profusely in small, compact clusters on pendulous branches. This graceful shrub is very beautiful when in full bloom. Even when out of bloom, its pendulous habit and foliage make it attractive.

Syringa japonica (Japanese Tree Lilac)—Japan.—This is a very satisfactory small tree or shrub, as it blooms so late and is tall and striking-looking.

Trees at the Experimental Farm, Ottawa, are, after thirty years' growth, some 20 feet in height, and about the end of June are a mass of creamy-white flowers. They are not perfumed, as the ordinary lilac is, but they are very handsome. *Syringa amurensis* is very similar.

Syringa villosa (Chinese Lilac)—North China.—This is a strong-growing lilac and is growing taller than at first expected, some specimens being now from 8 to 10 feet high. The leaves are rough and rather coarse-looking, but this tends to make the shrub more striking. It flowers during the second week of June, closely following *S. josikaea*. It is a free bloomer and the flowers, which are not highly perfumed, are bluish-pink and produced in good-sized panicles. This is a very desirable species. A hybrid between this and *S. josikaea* called Lutèce is a good hardy shrub. A hybrid between *S villosa* and *S. reflexa* originated in the Horticulture Division, Ottawa, is very promising.

Syringa vulgaris (Common Lilac)—Eastern Europe.—The common lilac and its varieties bloom during the first half of May, being usually at their best from the 20th to the 27th. There are many fine varieties of the lilac, varying in colour from white to the deepest purple. Some are single and some semi-double or double. Among the best are the following:—

Single:

Alba Grandiflora—white,
Aline Mocqueris—purplish-mauve, brighter in bud,
Congo—purplish-mauve, one of the deepest shades,
Decaisne—large, bluish lilac, very fine,
Delepin—bluish,
Jacques Calot—purplish-mauve in bud, violet mauve when opened, flowers large,
Lovaniensis—almost pink,
Toussaint-Louverture—bishop's violet, almost purple, one of the darkest in colour.

Double:

Charles Joly—vinous mauve, with twisted petals,
Comte de Kerchove—purplish-mauve changing to lighter shades,
Edith Cavell—flowers large, white, of good substance. A very fine white variety with large panicles of bloom,
Emile Lemoine—purplish-mauve changing to heliotrope,
Georges Bellair—purplish-mauve, petals tipped with white.
Hippolyte Maringer—lilac and bluish lilac effect, petals twisted.
Jean Bart—purplish-mauve to violet mauve, flowers with twisted petals,
Leon Gambetta—pinkish lilac, large panicle,
Madame Abel Chatenay—white,
Madame Casimir Perier—white,
Marc Micheli—violet mauve changing to heliotrope and white, flowers large,
Michel Buchner—violet mauve to bluish-violet,
Olivier de Serres—bluish lilac, large panicle,
Paul Thirion—later than most, rosy in bud, lilac when open,
President Fallières—pinkish lilac, late,
President Viger—rosy in bud, lilac when opened, changing to pinkish,
Wm. Robinson—rosy lilac in bud, lilac when open.

Two other fine hardy lilacs which should be in every collection are *S. rothomagensis* and *S. pubescens*.

Tamarix pentandra (Summer Tamarisk)—Southeast Europe to Central Asia.—A very pretty tamarisk, blooming from July until late summer. The flowers are small and pinkish in colour. It makes a very useful and graceful shrub and grows from 4 to 6 feet in height.

Viburnum (Native Viburnum).—There are several native species of Viburnum, in addition to the High Bush Cranberry, treated separately, which are very satisfactory shrubs on account of their ornamental flowers and foliage and because they will succeed in rather shady places where many other shrubs will not. Perhaps the most attractive of these is *V. cassinoides* or Withe-Rod, which blooms in June. This grows from 5 to 10 feet in height. Other taller species are: *V, lentago*, the Sheep Berry, and *V. prunifolium*, the Black Haw. All of these have white flowers and attractive foliage. The Arrow-wood, *Viburnum dentatum*, is also quite attractive and distinct in habit and foliage from the others. A good group of native Viburnums makes a very interesting and attractive feature of any ornamental grounds, and they are particularly useful where there is already some natural shrubbery.

Viburnum lantana (Wayfaring Tree)—Europe.—Height 8 to 12 feet. In bloom third week of May. Flowers white in compact, flat heads. The fruit is very ornamental, being scarlet, turning to dark purple when ripe.

Viburnum opulus (Guelder Rose, High Bush Cranberry)—Europe.— Height 6 to 8 feet. In bloom second week of June. Flowers white, in large clusters. This is, at all seasons of the year, an ornamental shrub, as the abundant bright scarlet fruit remains on the bush all winter. The native species, *V. americanum*, is also a very good ornamental shrub. *V. sargenti* is handsomer in bloom than either of the above but the fruit is not so attractive.

Viburnum opulus sterile (Snowball)—Height 8 to 10 feet. In bloom second week in June. The almost round clusters of pure white flowers of this shrub are well known. This is one of the most ornamental hardy flowering shrubs but for many years it has been badly attacked by aphis. To destroy these it is necessary to spray the bushes just as the buds are breaking in the spring. This is very important as at this time the eggs are hatching. A second spraying should be given in a few days and while the leaves are still only partly expanded. Once the insects cause the leaves to curl it is almost impossible to get at them. Kerosene emulsion, whale-oil soap, or nicotine preparations may be used for spraying.

LIST OF TWELVE MOST SATISFACTORY ORNAMENTAL SHRUBS OR GROUPS OF SHRUBS IN ORDER OF BLOOMING, AND COVERING THE SEASON WELL

Spiraea arguta
Spiraea van houttei
Caragana frutex var. *grandiflora*
Lonicera tatarica and varieties
Lilacs
Viburnum opulus

Philadelphus or Mock Orange
Roses
Robinia hispida
Hydrangea arborescens grandiflora
Hydrangea paniculata grandiflora
Tamarix pentandra

Deciduous Trees, Shrubs and Climbers with Attractive Foliage, Bark or Fruit

Many Canadians are establishing places in the country with the idea of either spending the greater part of the year there, or, at least, a few months; and there is an increasing interest in making places, both in town and country, especially attractive at all seasons of the year. As autumn is one of the most enjoyable seasons in Canada the fine landscape effects which can be obtained from form of tree, foliage, bark, or fruit should be carefully considered, and everything possible be done to make the landscape attractive at that season of the year.

The following notes are given in addition to others, which will be found elsewhere in this bulletin, in the hope that they will lead to a special effort being made at many places to make the autumn effects good. Some of the plants recommended for this purpose are very useful earlier in the season for their bloom and attractive foliage.

Acer (Maple).—It is scarcely necessary to tell Canadians of the beauty of the autumn colouring of our maples, but although we see this beauty as we wander through the woods or along the streets one often fails to plant these fine trees near the home. During the latter part of summer odd trees of the Red Maple (*Acer rubrum*) stand out among their duller surroundings clothed in scarlet and crimson, and a little later on this tree fairly makes the woods on fire with its bright coloured foliage. Still a little later, the leaves of the Hard Maple (*Acer saccharum*) take on their varied and attractive shades of red, green and yellow, and although the colours are not as bright as on the Red Maple they are often

Arborvitae hedge and Virginia Creeper.

richer. The Silver Maple (*Acer saccharinum*) is also very attractive, the green, yellow and bronze shades predominating. The most attractive maple not native to Canada is the Amur Maple (*Acer ginnala*). This little tree is ablaze with colour every year, no matter what the season is like, and rivals the Red Maple for brightness; scarlet, yellow, and crimson being the predominating colours. In the spring the Schwedler Maple (*Acer platanoides schwedleri*) is a very attractive tree, the young leaves being of a dark purplish crimson and contrasting well with the surrounding foliage of other trees. This tree soon loses its spring colouring, however, and the leaves become dull green. The Reitenbach Maple (*Acer platanoides reitenbachi*) another purple-leaved variety, while not as attractive in spring as the Schwedler Maple, retains its colour better throughout the summer.

Berberis (Barberry).—The barberries are very useful for autumn effect, as their foliage and fruit are both attractive. Among the best of these are: the Japanese Barberry (*Berberis thunbergi*), which grows about 4 feet high. It is a compact shrub with bright green foliage in summer which changes to deep red in autumn. The purple or red-leaved variety of this is desirable. The scarlet fruit is very abundant and makes this barberry quite ornamental throughout the winter. Another species (*Berberis sinensis*) is also very attractive both in foliage and fruit, and the Common Barberry (*Berberis vulgaris*) is also good. The purple-leaved variety of the latter species is one of the best purple-leaved shrubs and is very attractive. The Oregon Grape or Holly-leaved Barberry is a very desirable low-growing shrub with thick glossy, holly-like foliage, which becomes bronzy purple in the autumn.

Betula (Birch).—The yellow foliage of most of the Birches contrasts strongly with other trees in autumn, but the most attractive of all is the Cutleaf Weeping Birch (*Betula alba laciniata pendula*), the finely cut leaves and graceful form of which make it one of the most attractive trees. There is a purple-leaved variety of the White Birch, but the purple is rather dull and the tree, not especially desirable.

Caragana arborescens (Siberian Pea Tree).—This shrub has many points of merit and its bright, green compound leaves and fruiting pods give it a place in such a list as this.

Catalpa.—The Catalpas have such large foliage, suggestive of a sub-tropic climate, that it renders them especially attractive in the colder parts of the country, where they give a warmer tone to the landscape. The Japanese Catalpa (*Catalpa kaempferi*) is the hardiest species, but the Western Catalpa (*Catalpa speciosa*), though not as hardy, is more attractive and more desirable for the warmer parts of Ontario.

Celastrus (Shrubby Bitter-sweet).—There are two species of Shrubby Bitter-sweet which are especially desirable for their attractive fruit. The first is the native Climbing Bitter-sweet (*Celastrus scandens*). This is a very satisfactory hardy climber. The leaves are bright-green and free from insects and in the autumn and throughout the winter the scarlet-and-orange berries, which are produced in great abundance, make the vine very attractive. The outside of the berries is orange, but when they are cracked open by frost the scarlet inside is shown. The Japanese species (*Celestrus orbiculatus*) is just as attractive as the native one, and perhaps more so. The berries are smaller, but more abundant, and there is a greater contrast between the outside and inside, the outside being yellow and the inside orange. These vines may be kept quite shrub-like by cutting them back.

Cornus (Dogwood).—The hardy Dogwoods are most attractive in winter when the colour of the bark is much intensified. The best variety is *Cornus alba sibirica*, the bark of which is bright red in winter and in striking contrast with the snow, and other surrounding objects. There is a yellow barked variety of *Cornus stolonifera, flaviramea*, which could be used with good effect in contrast with the red-barked varieties. In foliage the most attractive hardy kind is *Cornus alba sibirica elegantissima* of the nursery catalogues, the leaves of, which are delicately variegated with white, silver and green, making this one of the best of variegated shrubs.

Contoneaster.—There are several hardy ornamental species of Cotoneasters. The species with the most attractive foliage is *C. acutifolia*, the dark, glossy green leaves of which make this shrub quite attractive. Among red fruited species, *C. racemiflora, C. tomentosa,* and *C. integerrima (vulgaris)* are the most desirable.

Crataegus (Hawthorn).—Some of the Hawthorns are attractive in flower, leaf and fruit; among these, two of the best are: *Crataegus coccinea* and *C. crusgalli*. Both of these species have glossy foliage and bright-red fruit, but the latter is, perhaps, preferable, as it does not sucker like the former, which may become troublesome.

Elaeagnus (Olive).—The Russian Olive (*Elaeagnus angustifolia*) is one of the best trees with silvery foliage, and is a very handsome species. The Wolf Willow *(E. argentea)* has a finer silvery foliage than the last, but as this species suckers badly it should be planted with caution.

Euonymus (Spindle Tree).—The different species of Euonymus do not, as a rule, make graceful or attractive shrubs at any time except autumn. At that season of the year, however, they are quite noticeable on account of their scarlet and red fruit, which is in some species very bright. The most attractive in fruit are *Euonymus europaeus* and *E. americanus*, but for brilliantly coloured foliage *E. atropurpureus* and *E. alatus* are excellent, and the fruit of these is also attractive.

Fagus (Beech).—The purple-leaved Beech (*Fagus sylvatica purpurea*) is one of the handsomest of trees where it is hardy, but unfortunately it kills back to the snow-line at Ottawa. The foliage is rich, bronzy purple and very attractive.

Ginkgo (Maiden-hair Tree).—*Ginkgo biloba*, is a very striking object in summer with its leaves suggesting those of the maiden-hair fern, and in autumn the leaves turn a very attractive yellow.

Hippophae rhamnoides (Sea buckthorn).—This is a hardy shrub with fairly attractive narrow leaves, which bears an abundant crop of small bright-orange fruit. It suckers badly and should be planted with discretion.

Ilex (Holly).—None of the Hollies are satisfactory at Ottawa, with the exception of the Black Alder *(Ilex verticillata)*. This shrub is not attractive during the summer, but in the autumn the scarlet holly-like fruit is very showy. There is a yellow-fruited variety of this which is also good.

Larix.—The leaves of the different species of Larch turn yellow in the autumn and make a pleasing contrast with the greens of the evergreens. The foliage is attractive in summer also.

Lonicera (Honeysuckle).—Many of the Honeysuckles are attractive, both in flower and fruit, but the best showy species when in fruit is *Lonicera tatarica*, and the many varieties of it. The fruit of this species varies in colour from yellow to bright red and shows up well in contrast with the foliage. Of the hardy climbing species the most attractive in foliage and fruit are those with glaucous foliage, such as *L. glauca, L. sullivanti*, and *L. flava*.

Lycium (Matrimony Vine).—The Matrimony Vine is very useful for training over rocks, stumps, and other places. The foliage is not especially attractive, but the numerous bright-scarlet berries in autumn are very showy.

Physocarpus (Ninebark).—The ordinary Ninebark (*Physocarpus opulifolius*) is not a very attractive shrub, although the seed pods are rather showy, but the golden leaved variety, *Neillia opulifolia aurea*, is a very striking object, and where a strong-growing, golden-leaved shrub is desired it is one of the best.

Pachysandra terminalis.—This is a dwarf, hardy shrub with attractive evergreen foliage, and succeeds well in shady places and is useful for ground cover.

Philadelphus.—The golden-leaved variety of the Mock Orange or Syringa. *Philadelphus coronarius*, is one of the best hardy golden-leaved shrubs.

Populus (Poplar).—The poplars have nearly all more or less attractive foliage, but probably the most attractive is the silver or white poplar, *Populus alba*, the leaves of which are silvery above and white below. The poplar multiplies rapidly by means of suckers, and as the falling seeds are disagreeable only trees with male flowers should be planted. A pyramidal variety, *Populus* *alba bolleana*, is a striking tree. The golden-leaved poplar, *Populus serotina aurea* (Van Geerti) is a good golden-leaved variety, but is much subject to galls. A weeping variety, *Populus grandidentata pendula*, is a very graceful tree with good foliage, and is especially handsome in flower.

Prunus (Plum).—The native plums of Canada and the United States are very attractive in flower and fruit, and, if varieties are chosen which have particularly attractive fruit, they may be used very advantageously.

Ptelea trifoliata aurea (Golden Hoptree).—This is one of the finest hardy golden-leaved shrubs. There is a richness of colour in this variety which is not excelled.

Pyrus (Sorbus) (Mountain Ash).—The Mountain Ashes are attractive both in flower and fruit, but are especially noticeable in autumn and winter when the bright-coloured fruit hangs thickly on the trees. The European Mountain Ash or Rowan Tree, *Pyrus aucuparia*, is perhaps the best, although the native Showy Mountain Ash, *Pyrus decora*, is good.

Pyrus (Crab Apple, Apple).—The Crab Apples and Apples make very showy trees, both in flower and fruit. One of the most useful Crab Apples is the wild Siberian Crab, *Pyrus baccata*. As this does not grow large it can be planted where other trees would be too large. The Redvein Crab Apple *(Pyrus niedzwetzkyana)* has attractive reddish-purple foliage and rose-coloured flowers.

Quercus (Oak).—The oaks keep up the show of colour in the autumn after most of the other trees have lost their leaves. The two most desirable hardy species are the Red Oak, *Quercus rubra*, and the Black Oak, *Quercus velutina*. Both of these species colour up well in autumn and the leaves remain bright until severe frosts. The Scarlet Oak, *Quercus coccinea*, though not quite as hardy, colours well also. The laurel-like leaves of *Quercus imbricaria* are very attractive in summer.

Rhus (Sumac).—Sumacs are among the most showy autumn tinted shrubs and trees, and are very effective when grown wild in large masses. The common native species, the Staghorn Sumac, *Rhus typhina*, is one of the best and its compound leaves tinted with red are very striking. The Smooth Sumac, *Rhus glabra*, and the graceful cut-leaved variety of it are also fine. The foliage of the low-growing fragrant Sumac, *Rhus aromatica*, always colours well and there is a richness of tints in it not found in the others. The Smoke Tree, *Rhus cotinus*, is a very striking shrub. The pedicels in the loose flowering panicles become covered with soft hairs which give a smoke-like effect to the whole plant. The leaves also colour well and are attractive both in summer and autumn.

Ribes alpinum (Mountain Currant).—This is quite a showy species with bright-red fruit and deep green glossy leaves.

Rosa (rose).—The wild roses are nearly all effective when in bloom, and some have attractive foliage and fruit. One of the best wild roses in foliage and fruit is *Rosa lucida*. This species has glossy leaves which contrast well with the red fruit. The Japanese Rose, *Rosa rugosa*, has very ornamental foliage and fruit, the leaves being rich green and glossy and the fruit of large size and very striking. Another good species is *Rosa pomifera*, which has exceptionally large fruit and silvery or glaucous leaves. The Redleaf Rose, *Rosa rubrifolia*, is one of the best reddish-leaved shrubs. The leaves are deep reddish purple, and when the shrub is in bloom the contrast between the leaves and delicate pink flowers is very good.

Englemann Virginia Creeper on the left; Self-fastening Virginia Creeper on right. The latter clings much better than the former.

Salix (Willow).—There are quite a number of Willows which have ornamental leaves and bark and in the winter those with attractive bark are especially noticeable, and brighten up the landscape very much. The Laurel-leaved Willow, *Salix pentandra (laurifolia)*, is a very ornamental tree, the leaves being deep green and very glossy. The rosemary-leaved Willow, *Salix rosmarinifolia*, has narrow, rosemary-like leaves, and where a shrubby Willow is desired it is one of the best. The best Willows with attractive bark are: *Salix alba britzensis*, with red bark, and *S. alba vitellina flava* or *S. voronesh* with a yellow bark. These varieties are in striking contrast and stand out well in a winter landscape, as do the weeping forms.

Sambucus (Elder).—Some of the elders are quite desirable. One of the best gold-leaved shrubs is *Sambucus canadensis aurea*. The European Red Elder, *Sambucus racemosa*, and its varieties may be used with good effect.

Spiræa.—There are a few hardy spiræas with good foliage, among these being *Spiræa van houttei*, also one of the best when in bloom; *Spiræa arguta*, also one of the best when in bloom; *Spiræa thunbergi*, not quite hardy at Ottawa, and *Spiræa sorbifolia*.

Symphoricarpus (Snowberry).—The Snowberry, *Symphoricarpus racemosus*, is well known, the pure-white berries in autumn being a familiar sight in most parts of Canada. The Coral Berry, *Symphoricarpus vulgaris*, which has red fruit, is also effective, especially when in contrast with the other.

Tamarix amurensis.—This Tamarisk is the hardiest of all those tested, and although it kills back some it makes strong growth during the summer. It is an elegant shrub with small foliage and tender branchlets. The *Tamarix pentandra (aestivalis)* is very effective all the season and it blooms in summer.

Viburnum (Arrow-wood).—The Viburnums are nearly all attractive shrubs in flower and foliage, and some species have very ornamental fruit. The Guelder Rose or High-bush Cranberry, *Viburnum opulus*, is probably the most satisfactory. It is beautiful when in bloom, the foliage is effective, and the scarlet fruit which hangs on nearly or quite all winter makes it very desirable. Next will come the Wayfaring Tree, *Viburnum lantana*. This also has ornamental flowers, foliage and fruit. Unlike the Guelder Rose, however, the fruit does not hang long. When ripening, the fruit is at first scarlet and becomes black when fully ripe. Two other species with very attractive foliage are: *Viburnum prunifolium* and *Viburnum dentatum*, both native species.

Ampelopsis (Virginia Creeper).—The Virginia Creeper, *Ampelopsis quinquefolia*, is well known, but must appear in a list of this kind. The leaves, while quite attractive in summer, become highly coloured at the first approach of autumn and for some time this vine is very effective. The self-fastening variety colours as well and has the advantage of clinging unaided to the wall on which it is trained.

Perennial Climbing Plants

For many years a large number of kinds of climbing plants have been under test at the Central Experimental Farm, Ottawa, and much information obtained in regard to their relative hardiness, attractiveness and usefulness. There are many houses which could be made much more attractive-looking by the judicious use of some of these vines. A house which lacks any pretence of beauty in architecture may have much of the stiffness taken from it by planting a vine where it will break the monotony of a straight wall. Verandahs, summer-houses, fences, rocks and old stumps of trees covered with climbing plants will so change the appearance of a place that it will hardly be recognized by one who has known it before. There are so many good, hardy, native climbers that it is not necessary to go to any expense in procuring something which will produce the desired effect. In the following list of vines found most satisfactory at Ottawa are a number of native plants.

Climbers usually make rapid growth when once established. The best results will be obtained, however, by preparing the ground well beforehand. Usually the soil about buildings is poor, and, if such be the case, it will well repay anyone to remove it where the vines are to be planted and replace it with some of a good loamy character, thoroughly mixing well-rotted manure with it. If such preparation is given the results will almost certainly be satisfactory.

The following perennial climbers all have woody stems except the Wild Hop, Kudzu Vine and Perennial Pea:—

Ampelopsis quinquefolia (Virginia Creeper).—This native climber, also known as *Parthenocissus quinquefolia, Psedera quinquefolia* and *Vitis quinquefolia,* is one of the most popular ornamental vines. It is a rapid grower and, being a native of the colder parts of Eastern Canada westward to Manitoba, is one of the hardiest. Its glossy, green leaves become very brilliant in autumn, when they assume many shades of red. Although it has tendrils by which it clings, if there are crevices into which they can be inserted, it will not cling to a wall where there are not such places and has to be supported in some other way. It is very desirable for training over summer houses, fences, verandahs, and even on walls, where it falls in graceful festoons and becomes very attractive. Unfortunately it is much subject to leaf-hoppers and, while there is a remedy in whale-oil soap, tobacco preparations or kerosene emulsion, they have to be applied very persistently and the work begun before the vines have become disfigured. Where there is a good circulation of air, or where the vines are often moved by the wind, they will not be so troublesome.

Ampelopsis quinquefolia engelmannii (Engelmann Virginia Creeper). —This variety has smaller foliage than the type and has discs on the tendrils by which it clings to walls, thus not needing to be provided with a special support as does the type. At times, however, such as when there is a high wind, these discs are not sufficient to hold the vines and they are blown down, hence the variety hirsuta, which is provided with more discs, is more satisfactory.

Ampelopsis quinquefolia hirsuta (Self-fastening Virginia Creeper or Hairy Virginia Creeper).—The Self-fastening Virginia Creeper is a very distinct variety found growing wild at Ottawa and other districts in Eastern Canada and, no doubt, in the United States. The leaves are smaller than the type and are distinguished from it also by being downy or hairy and are of a duller colour in summer, though they become bright red in autumn. Its great value lies in its having discs on the short tendrils by which it clings tightly to brick, stone, concrete, or wood, hence needs no special support. Moreover, the downiness of the leaves is evidently unpleasant to the leaf-hopper, as there is usually little or no injury.

Ampelopsis tricuspidata (Japanese Ivy or Boston Ivy).—Other names for this excellent climber or creeper are *Ampelopsis veitchi, Parthenocissus tricuspidata* and *Vitis inconstans.* The Japanese Ivy is not quite hardy enough in Eastern Ontario. Occasional vines at Ottawa develop well, but it kills back more or less every year and sometimes is killed out altogether. In the warmest parts of Canada, however, it is grown with good success. It is a beautiful vine and clings so tightly to the wall on which it is trained that it is unsurpassed in this regard. The leaves are of an attractive green in summer and, at times, are highly coloured in autumn. When grown in those parts of Canada where it kills back badly in winter a north or west exposure is desirable. The thawing and freezing which it often gets on a south side in early spring is very hard on it. It is desirable to protect the lower part of the vine with sacking, or wood with straw underneath, which will better ensure part of the plant coming through safely.

Aristolochia sipho (Dutchman's Pipe).—Although this fine climber is somewhat slow in becoming established and usually does not make much growth for two or three years, once it is well rooted it grows very rapidly and becomes one of the most beautiful and striking hardy vines available. The leaves are large, heart-shaped and deep green and give a semi-tropical effect. It has a heavier look than some other vines and seems in keeping rather with the more massive style of verandah than that of lighter design. It is of a twining habit and looks well on either a trellis or verandah. The flowers, which are partially hidden by the large leaves, are brown and of a peculiar shape, much resembling a Dutchman's pipe. It is a native of the Eastern States and grows from twenty to thirty feet or more high.

Celastrus orbiculatus (Japanese Bittersweet).—Although the native species is very attractive, this, in some respects, is still more so, as the fruits are smaller, more numerous, and the whole effect more graceful. It is, however, after the leaves have fallen that the fruit is so noticeable, as before that time, that of the native Climbing Bittersweet is, perhaps, more conspicuous. There is a greater contrast between the outside and inside of the fruit of the Japanese than there is in *Celastrus scandens*, the colours being distinct yellow and orange. This is a native of Japan and China. It is quite hardy, is a rapid grower and very desirable, especially for covering fences. One should be sure of getting a plant having both male and female flowers to ensure having a crop of fruit.

Celastrus scandens (American Bittersweet, Wax-work).—This is one of the best native climbers. It is a very rapid, even rampant grower, with glossy green leaves and highly ornamental fruit, and very suitable for training over summer houses and verandahs as it twines about everything it can get hold of. It is particularly free from injurious insects and diseases. In the autumn and early winter, after the leaves have fallen, the attractiveness of this vine is continued by the orange coloured fruit or berries which, after the early frosts, crack open, revealing a scarlet interior. In procuring this vine one should get one which is known to fruit or has been propagated from one that is known to fruit, as some vines have only male blossoms and there is no fruit on such.

Clematis jackmani (Jackman Clematis).—This is the most satisfactory of the large-flowered Clematis. It is a very free bloomer and remains in flower for several weeks. The flowers are very large and rich violet purple in colour, with a velvety appearance. Where a strong colour effect is desired this is a good plant to use. There are many large-flowered hybrid clematis and a good range in colour can easily be obtained. The chief defect in these varieties is that they are subject to the injury known as collar rot, especially the first year or two after setting out, but once they become well established they usually thrive well.

Clematis ligusticifolia (Western Virgin's Bower).—The Western Virgin's Bower is a native of the drier districts of Western Canada and the United States, and when grown in Eastern Canada it should be planted in as dry a situation as possible. It is particularly valuable in the Prairie Provinces, where the number of hardy perennial climbers is limited and where the summers are relatively dry. There it makes an excellent climber for a trellis on the verandah or house and reaches a height of 20 feet or more. The leaves are glossy and attractive in appearance and these, combined with the numerous small white flowers which this native vine bears, make it a very desirable plant, especially for the colder and drier parts of Canada.

Clematis paniculata (Japanese Clematis).—This clematis, which is also called Sweet Autumn Clematis because of its sweet-scented flowers, is a very ornamental climber, and because it blooms in September is particularly valuable where it succeeds well. A warm and well-drained situation is best for it. At Ottawa it often kills out if not given some protection before winter sets in and is really not as generally satisfactory as in the warmer districts. The flowers are larger and whiter than most of the other small-flowered species. When it succeeds well it reaches a height of fifteen feet or more. It is a native of Japan.

Clematis virginiana (Virgin's Bower).—The Virgin's Bower is a common native climber in Eastern Canada and is not used as much as it should be for beautifying the home. Next to the Virginia Creeper it is, perhaps, the most satisfactory native climber to plant, and where Virginia Creepers are badly affected with leaf-hoppers or thrips it may give better satisfaction than the latter. It is a very rapid grower and soon covers anything it is planted near, reaching a height of twenty feet or more. It clings by tendrils and should have something to which these can fasten.

Clematis vitalba (Traveller's Joy).—The Traveller's Joy is an European species very much like the Virgin's Bower, and where the latter cannot be obtained the Traveller's Joy is a good substitute. It is even a stronger grower than the Virginia Creeper and reaches a height of from twenty to thirty feet.

Humulus lupulus (Common Hop).—The Common Hop is used more in the Prairie Provinces as a climber about the house than in any other part of Canada. It is a native of the prairies and very hardy and makes rapid growth from the ground each year. It is not, however, as attractive a vine as some others, but where the number of hardy vines is limited the common hop is not to be despised. It makes an excellent screen from the sun during the hot weather.

Lathyrus latifolius (Perennial Pea).—While not a tall climber the Perennial Pea is quite satisfactory if one does not desire a vine which grows more than 8 or 9 feet high. While the flowers are not sweet-scented, they are very attractive and of great substance and are usually in bloom before the Sweet Pea. The white and pale pink shades are among the most attractive.

Lonicera hirsuta (Hairy Honeysuckle).—There are several native climbing Honeysuckles, but this is perhaps the best of them. It bears attractive orange-yellow flowers during the month of June. It is not, however, as satisfactory a climber as the Scarlet Trumpet Honeysuckle, as its blooming season is soon over.

Lonicera japonica halliana (Hall Japanese Honeysuckle).—This Honeysuckle is not hardy at Ottawa, but is often planted, as it is much recommended when it succeeds, as it does in the warmest parts of Canada. The flowers are small white, turning to yellow. Where hardy it blooms well during the latter part of summer.

Lonicera periclymenum (Woodbine, English Honeysuckle). Because of the agreeable, spicy odour of its flowers and its association with the Old Land this is a very popular climber with many where it succeeds well. At Ottawa, however, it has not proved very hardy and usually there are but few flowers and occasionally the vines are killed out altogether.

Lonicera sempervirens (Scarlet Trumpet Honeysuckle).—No other Honeysuckle has proved as desirable at Ottawa as this one. It blooms almost continuously from the first week of June until late in the autumn and the bright scarlet, trumpet-shaped flowers, which are borne profusely, are very effective. It is a native of the Eastern United States and almost perfectly hardy at Ottawa.

Lycium chinense (Chinese Matrimony-Vine).—Where a tall-growing climber is not desired and something is needed for covering rocks, stumps or trees this is very useful. While neither the leaves nor flowers are particularly ornamental, the graceful habit of the plant commends it, together with the fact that in the autumn the bright scarlet fruit gives it a very attractive appearance. The European or common Matrimony-Vine (*Lycium europaeum*) is a desirable climber also, but is not so good as *L. chinense*, as the fruit is smaller and the foliage not so attractive.

Pueraria hirsuta (Kudzu Vine).—The Kudzu vine is one of the fastest and strongest growing climbing plants and will make a growth of from forty to fifty feet in one season when conditions are favourable. It has not proven hardy at Ottawa and is only suited to the warmest parts of Canada and is really too rampart a grower to be very satisfactory even when it does succeed. It is a native of Japan.

Roses—Climbing Varieties.—The climbing Roses give wonderfully charming effects in the garden and about the house and, as hardier sorts are originated, their use will. no doubt, become much more general than it is at present. Now, the climbing Roses that are available have all to be protected in winter at Ottawa and other places where the winters are as severe. Even when protected there are many which are not satisfactory, but the following have proved among the hardiest and most reliable: American Pillar, Crimson Rambler, Dorothy Perkins, Dr. Van Fleet, Euphrosyne, Evangeline, Hiawatha, Mrs. F. W. Flight, Tausendschon, Chatillon.

Vitis vulpina (Riverbank Grape).—The Riverbank Grape is very hardy and grows wild as far west as Manitoba. It makes an ornamental climber and is a very rapid grower. The male and female flowers of this species are grown on different vines and to have the delightful perfume of the flowers, for which this species and other grapes are noted, one with male flowers should be planted. However, by having two vines, one with male and the other with female flowers, planted close together, one could have both the perfume and the fruit. One draw-back to having the Wild Grape used as a climber near the house is that it is subject to the attacks of leaf-hoppers, which often disfigure the leaves. In exposed places, however, where there is a good circulation of air, they will not be so troublesome.

Wisteria sinensis (Chinese Wisteria).—This beautiful climber is not hardy at Ottawa without protection, but if planted in a naturally protected place and the vine laid down and protected before the winter sets in, it will bloom fairly well and is of such striking beauty when in bloom that a little special effort is well worth while. If left unprotected the wood will withstand the cold, or there will be very little killing back, but the flower buds are killed and there will be no bloom.

Other climbers to which reference should be made, which are not hardy at Ottawa, but which succeed in the milder parts of Canada, are the English Ivy (*Hedera helix*), the Trumpet Creeper (*Campsis radicans, Bignonia radicans, Tecoma radicans*), *Euonymus radicans vegeta* and the *Actinidia arguta*.

There are a few fine vines of English ivy on the Niagara peninsula, but it is not hardy at Ottawa. It is one of the few very good evergreen climbers and a hardy form of this would be very desirable.

The Trumpet Creeper makes strong growth each year at Ottawa, but is killed back badly each year and does not bloom well at all, although it has bloomed there. It is a native of the Eastern States, but extending south, and plants from the coldest part of its range are most likely to succeed. In some places in southwestern Ontario it blooms satisfactorily.

The evergreen climber or creeper known as *Euonymus radicans vegeta* is considered a little hardier than the English ivy and if it proves generally so will be a welcome addition, but this Euonymus is not hardy where the climate is as cold as Ottawa.

A Chinese vine known as *Actinidia arguta* is a very strong grower and has attractive fruit, but is only suitable for the warmest parts of Canada. It kills back badly at Ottawa.

Another very attractive climber when in full bloom is *Polygonum baldschuanicum*, or Silver Fleecevine. The many small, pink and whitish, buckwheat-like flowers borne during the summer months give a very graceful appearance to this vine, which will grow to 20 feet in height. Unfortunately it is not quite hardy enough at Ottawa, being killed out from time to time.

Hedges

There appears to be a growing interest in hedges in Canada and, if there is, the Experimental Farms should receive credit for much valuable experimental work which has been done in the past forty years in testing trees and shrubs for hedge purposes in different parts of Canada. At practically all of the Dominion Experimental Farms and Stations there are sample hedges which have attracted much attention from visitors.

The collection of hedges at the Central Experimental Farm, Ottawa, is, so far as the writer is aware, the largest in the world. There are now eighty-four hedges, each fifty feet in length, most of which are growing side by side so that they can be readily compared. In all some one hundred and twenty species of trees and shrubs have been tested.

The plants for each of these hedges were set in a row 18 inches apart, which has been found a satisfactory method on the whole. It has been found best in starting a hedge to use small plants from 1½ to 3 feet in height. The soil for the plants is first dug and levelled or raked and, if thought necessary, well-rotted manure is thoroughly incorporated with it before planting, but no manure is put in the trench which is opened for the plants. Usually it has not been necessary to use any manure at the time of planting, as the soil is fairly good. The trees are planted a little deeper, say from 1 to 2 inches, than they had been in the nursery from which they came. This is to provide for some heaving the first winter and also to make certain that they are not planted too shallow. Early spring planting both for evergreens and deciduous species has been found the best and summer planting of evergreens is not recommended. The soil should be tramped in well about the roots so as to ensure their quick contact with moist soil. After planting the plants should be pruned back to the same height if they are uneven in growth.

The hedges at Ottawa are pruned regularly each year, the usual time for pruning being after most of the growth has been made. For some sorts this is early in June, whereas for others it is late in June or early July. By pruning at this time there is usually a little more growth made which covers the wounds made in pruning and the hedge looks neat until nearly the same time next year. Some kinds require a second pruning late in summer as odd shoots grow up which should be removed to keep the hedge looking neat, and with a few sorts there is a fairly strong second growth.

The shape of hedge which has been found most pleasing to the eye and at the same time ensures the branches remaining alive almost or quite to the ground is one with the broadest part of the hedge at the ground, gradually narrowing towards the top, but the top being rounded instead of being pruned to a sharp point.

While a large number of species have been tried those which are satisfactory for many years are relatively few. The chief defect of most of the hedges is that they become too open at the base, while others require too much pruning.

Where a tall hedge is required one of the following might be used with good effect: Siberian Pea Tree, Honey Locust, Josika Lilac, Common Buckthorn. The White, Yellow and Black Birches have also made good hedges at Ottawa and stand pruning well.

Hedges at Central Experimental Farm, Ottawa.

Siberian Pea Tree (Caragana arborescens).—This is, perhaps, the best of all deciduous hedges for the colder parts of Canada. It is very hardy and a fast grower and its leaves, which come out very early, are of an attractive shade of green. As it makes practically all its growth early in the season one pruning each year is sufficient. This shrub-like tree will reach a height of 18 feet if desired. The Siberian Pea Tree should be in full sunlight for best results, as if shaded the bottom will become too open. This plant has attractive yellow pea-shaped flowers when not pruned. In recent years the foliage has been somewhat disfigured by leaf-hoppers.

Common Buckthorn (Rhamnus catharticus).—The Common Buckthorn makes a good tall hedge though the foliage is not so attractive as the Siberian Pea Tree. It is, however, a firmer hedge than the Caragana and where one is desired that will stand rather adverse conditions this is a good one. It stands pruning well. It will grow to any height desired for a hedge.

Honey Locust (Gleditschia triacanthos).—Where a hedge is desired that will hold small animals to a great extent the Honey Locust is one of the most satisfactory. It is very thorny and the thorns are long and sharp. It requires more pruning, however, than either of the two previously mentioned hedges and is not hardy enough for the coldest sections, though it has done very well at Ottawa.

Josika Lilac (Syringa josikaea).—Many persons like to have a Lilac hedge, mainly, as a matter of sentiment, for the Common Lilac is not a very satisfactory hedge plant, not being stiff enough nor having attractive enough foliage for a hedge which is to be looked at all the season. The foliage often becomes badly mildewed which makes it still less attractive and, when grown as a clipped hedge, there will be no flowers. The Josika Lilac, however, makes a much better hedge plant than the Common. The leaves are deep green in colour and glossy, and the bush is firmer than the other. It is one of the most attractive tall hedges at Ottawa.

TALL EVERGREEN HEDGES

The two most satisfactory tall evergreen hedges are the Douglas Fir and Norway Spruce, although the White Pine (*Pinus strobus*) has made an excellent hedge at Ottawa and is still in good condition though planted in 1890, over thirty-seven years ago. The Arborvitæ, or White Cedar, might be included with the tall hedges, as it will grow as tall as required, but it has been put with those of medium-height.

Douglas Fir (Pseudotsuga taxifolia).—This has proved to be the best tall evergreen hedge at Ottawa. Planted in 1894 this sample hedge is still in excellent condition, as is also another hedge of it planted before that time, and has living branches to the ground. The foliage is attractive and the hedge looks well.

Norway Spruce (Picea excelsa).—This is a very fast-growing spruce, but is only fairly satisfactory as a hedge plant where one is looking for a hedge that will stay in good condition for a long time. For the first ten or fifteen years it may do well, but later on the lower branches are likely to die unless it is under very favourable conditions. It is such a strong grower also that it needs much pruning to keep it within bounds. This Spruce should be in the open where it will get bright light to do its best. The native White Spruce (*Picea canadensis*) makes a beautiful hedge, but is so often disfigured by the Spruce-gall worm that it is not recommended for general planting on this account.

DECIDUOUS HEDGES OF MEDIUM HEIGHT

A few satisfactory hedges of medium to tall-growing shrubs have been found among the many that have been tested. Two of the best are the Alder Buckthorn and Wayfaring Tree. The Shrubby or Woody Caragana (*Caragana frutescens*) makes an attractive looking hedge, but is rather soft and sometimes gets out of shape with the weight of snow. It also suckers to some extent. The Tamarack and European Larch have both made good hedges.

Alder Buckthorn (Rhamnus frangula).—This is a more attractive-looking hedge than the Common Buckthorn. The leaves are rather small, are glossy and of an attractive shade of green. It stands pruning well and will succeed in partial shade better than some others. While put among hedges of medium height, if allowed to grow, it will reach any height a hedge is likely to be needed, but can be kept down with little trouble. It is not thorny like the Common Buckthorn and on this account is not so desirable where anything is liable to run up against it much.

Wayfaring Tree (Viburnum lantana).—The Wayfaring Tree, or shrub, as it really is, was planted as a hedge in 1890 and after thirty-seven years is still in good condition. While the foliage is rather large to make the most attractive kind of hedge, it is of a lively green colour which offsets that to a large extent. It has done well under pruning and is still clothed with branches to the ground. While the hedge at Ottawa is in bright light, this shrub would probably succeed better in partial shade than some others.

The best evergreen hedges of medium height are those made by the various forms of the American Arborvitæ, but the ordinary one found growing wild in many places in Eastern Canada is very satisfactory. The Japanese Yew (*Taxus cuspidata*) is promising and the Swiss Stone Pine (*Pinus cembra*) is still a good hedge after twenty-six years' growth.

American Arborvitæ (Thuja occidentalis).—This is the best evergreen hedge which can be readily kept at a medium height, or let grow tall as desired. It stands clipping well, will endure shade better than most plants, is only a moderately strong grower, lessening the amount of pruning which would otherwise be necessary, and can readily be kept looking well trimmed for most of the year. It is also very hardy. The hardiest variety of this would seem to be the Siberian Arborvitæ (*Thuja occidentalis wareana*), which, however, has a little coarser look than the ordinary form. Other varieties are dwarfer and they are very suitable where a low-growing evergreen hedge is desired. Among these may be mentioned the Globose Arborvitæ (*Thuja occidentalis globosa*) and Compact Arborvitæ (*Thuja occidentalis compacta*).

LOW-GROWING DECIDUOUS HEDGES

Three of the best low-growing hardy deciduous hedges are the Japanese Barberry (*Berberis thunbergi*), the Dwarf Caragana (*Caragana pygmœa*) and the Alpine Currant (*Ribes alpinum*). The only privet that has proved at all suitable for hedge purposes at Ottawa is the Amur Privet (*Ligustrum amurense*), but from time to time even this kills to near the ground and the hedge becomes unsightly for a time, hence no privet is recommended for the colder parts of Ontario nor for Quebec.

Japanese Barberry (Berberis thunbergi):—This the most satisfactory and most popular low-growing hedge. It will reach a height of 4 feet if desired. It has the good hedge qualities of being compact in habit with small attractive foliage and sufficiently firm to keep its shape well. The leaves become highly coloured in autumn and after they fall the scarlet berries give this hedge a pleasing appearance until it is covered with snow. So far the disease which causes the rust of wheat has not been found on this species, so that it can be planted without fear of its doing harm. There is a dwarf form of this called Box Barberry, which should prove very useful where a very small hedge is desired. The purple or red-leaved variety is promising.

Dwarf Caragana (Caragana pygmæa).—Dwarf caragana, because of its great hardiness and attractive flowers, is a desirable shrub, but on account of its small foliage and neat habit it makes a very good low hedge. The colour of the foliage, however, is rather dull, which detracts from it where a bright-looking hedge is desired.

Alpine Currant (Ribes alpinum).—The Alpine Currant has not been tested long at Ottawa as a hedge plant, but it has done well elsewhere and it promises to make a good low hedge here. The foliage is comparatively small and is of an attractive shade of green, and the habit of the bush is compact.

OTTAWA: Printed by F. A. ACLAND, Printer to the King's Most Excellent Majesty, 1927.